GW01239158

WELCOME TO

THE MOST INSPIRING TENNIS STORIES FOR YOUNG READERS

Lunar Press is an independent publishing company that cares greatly about the accuracy of its content.

If you notice any inaccuracies or have anything that you would like to discuss, then please email us at lunarpresspublishers@gmail.com.

Enjoy!

COMPLETE THE SET!

Looking for your next read?

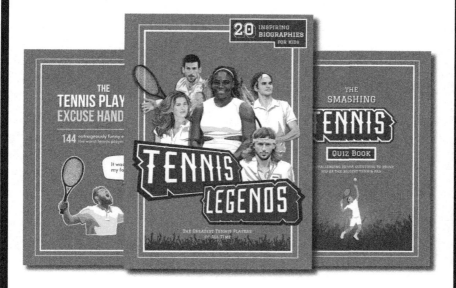

Tennis Legends is a collection of **20 illustrated biographies** of the best players to ever step onto the court and is a great way for young tennis fans to learn about the legends of the past.

The Smashing Tennis Quiz is a collection of **444 challenging trivia questions** - test yourself or compete with a family quiz night!

The Tennis Player's Excuse Handbook is **the perfect novelty gift** for tennis players of all abilities - get your copies today and complete your set of tennis books!

CONTENTS

Inspirational Stories

Fairytale Runs

Legendary Comebacks

Timeless Tennis Classics

WARM UP

Tennis has produced so many inspirational stories over the years that it would be impossible to fit them all into one book. In fact, anybody who makes it in professional sports of any kind is an inspiration! It's not easy to be the cream of the crop, especially in a sport as popular as tennis. The more popular a sport, the more people play it, which makes it harder to reach the top of the pile.

Tennis can be traced back as far as the 12th century, when a form of it was played in France. Back then, they used the palm of their hands to strike a small ball over a net. Rackets were added over time, which led to the version of tennis we love today.

Louis X (1289–1316), the king of France in the early 14th century, is said to have been a massive fan of a sport called jeu de paume ("game of the palm"), which was the early version of tennis mentioned above. He had indoor courts built in his castle, making them the first known indoor courts in history!

Between 1859 and 1865, two men named Harry Gem and Augurio Perera created new rules and regulations for the sport, which made it look a lot more like the modern version of tennis. They added rackets and lines and then began perfecting the game on Perera's croquet* court in Birmingham. By 1872, they had created the first tennis club in the world, and several other local sports people joined.

Tennis took off, and soon, it was known and played all over the world. It quickly became one of the biggest and most popular sports in history.

It seems that every decade in the 20th century saw legendary stories unfold. Different countries dominated during different periods, like France in the 1920s and '30s and America in the 1990s. There was the Navratilova-Graf rivalry in the 1980s and the McEnroe-Borg rivalry that same decade. Then, of course, the 2000s arrived, and it became all about the "Big Three" and the Williams sisters.

All of these legends and more will be covered in this book. Each of them had many memorable matches, great comebacks, inspirational stories, and brilliant rivalries. The best always bring the best out in one another. Bjorn Borg and John McEnroe hated each other back when they were world No. 1 and No. 2, but deep down, they both knew they needed each other. Alone, they might have taken their foot off the pedal and let their performances slip. Knowing the other one was breathing down their neck meant that they had to stay on it all the time with no let-ups!

The dominance of the Williams sisters will surely never be seen again. Two sisters, both amazing, and both playing in a way that had never been seen before. The odds of it happening again are just too slim. For one player like that to come along, maybe, but two? Tennis is all the better for having witnessed such brilliance.

The same can be said for Novak Djokovic, Rafael Nadal, and Roger Federer. How can three of the greatest players in history break through at pretty much the same time? How did all three still manage to win so many Slams when they had to face each other all the time? It goes to show how evenly matched they were and how blessed we were to see them play.

Inspiration comes in many ways, not just in sports. It can hit us as we watch our parents running around in the morning before sending us off to school. Seeing them make breakfast, get ready for work, pack our lunch, juggle a hundred different chores all at once, and make sure we brush our teeth is a sight to behold! It can be inspirational!

It can come from a friend who refuses to accept they aren't good enough to make the team, so they train and train and train until the coach simply can't refuse them anymore. Or it might be the teacher who continues to inspire, even when it seems like the class isn't paying attention.

All these things and more can inspire us, but is there anything like seeing a tennis player finishing an epic 30-shot rally with a huge forehand down the line to win the title? Watching them collapse to the court in tears as they finally get their hands on the trophy is amazing. Seeing how tired they are after a five-hour final but still so full of energy because they've put everything into the match can make the hairs on the back of your neck stand up.

Of course, tennis is one of the more inspiring sports for many reasons. One reason is the fact that players can break through much earlier than other sports. Kids as young as 13 or 14 have played in Slams. Coco Gauff, the Williams sisters, Monica Seles, Michael Chang, and so many more made the final and even won Slams before they turned 18! If that doesn't inspire us, then nothing will!

Tennis is also one of the most entertaining sports in the world. Because there is no time limit, matches can have many moments when it seems like it's all over, only for one player to save several match points in a couple of minutes. Suddenly, the momentum switches and the player we thought was sure to lose somehow brings the match level, and everything gets turned on its head!

Comebacks in tennis are brilliant. A player can be two sets down, playing awful, and constantly arguing with the umpire. A few moments later, something will switch in them, and before you know it, they've rattled off a handful of games, and their opponent starts to look worried. As we watch, we can almost feel the energy shifting. It's a wonderful thing to witness.

Now it's time for you to dive into these inspirational stories, which will be followed by some brilliant fairy-tale runs, quite a few shocking comebacks, a bunch of epic matches, and plenty of fun along the way!

INSPIRATIONAL
STORIES

ARTHUR ASHE'S
FIGHT FOR JUSTICE

Racism has existed throughout history, and sport is no different. Like football, baseball, athletics, and so many others, tennis also had a period when certain races weren't allowed to play. Thankfully, those days are long gone, and that has a lot to do with amazing people like Arthur Ashe.

Arthur achieved so many "firsts" in tennis, and all of them were important. He was the first black men's player to win a singles title at Wimbledon, the Australian Open, and the US Open. He was the first black player selected by the United States Davis Cup team (a competition he won four times!), and he was the first African American to be ranked No. 1!

Sadly, Arthur died when he was just 49, but in his short life, he changed the sport of tennis forever. He opened doors for future generations, and he was a true hero.

His story began on July 10, 1943, when he was born in Richmond, Virginia. The family didn't have much, and things got even harder when Arthur's mother died suddenly. He was just 6 when he lost her.

Arthur's father had to work several jobs while also raising a family. One of his jobs was as a caretaker at Brookfield Park, one of the only tennis clubs in America at the time that allowed black people to play.

Arthur's father was strict but fair with his kids. He told them that if they wanted to use the tennis and basketball courts at Brookfield, they had to do well in their studies to earn it. He knew that discipline and education were very important.

Growing up, Arthur wasn't the biggest kid. The family sometimes went hungry, so he was small and thin. He earned nicknames such as "Skinny" and "Bones," but he didn't mind. Instead, he decided to work on ways to better himself. If he was the skinniest kid, he could slip past people on the basketball court. If he was light, he could move faster than his opponent when he played tennis.

Arthur soon discovered that of all the sports he liked, he loved tennis the most. He was nimble* and agile*, so he could move around the court rapidly. This suited his serve and volley game, which would one day make him a tennis star! He spent every minute he could practicing.

His love of tennis started when he was about 7, and it never left him. He quickly became far better than his brothers and sisters and anyone else he played. He was soon spotted by a man named Ron Charity, who was known as the best black player in the state. Ron saw how good Arthur was and asked if he could coach the boy.

Ron taught Arthur that some of the most important things to learn in sports are not the talents and strengths you're born with—they're the mental skills you learn along the way. Discipline, humility*, and sportsmanship* make you a better person, and that helps you to reach your goals!

Throughout Arthur's early years as a young teenage star, he was often held back. Many tournaments refused to let him enter, and the ones that did soon changed their rules when he kept winning. This was all down to the color of his skin, and it hurt Arthur. He could have grown up bitter, but instead, he always tried to be kind and understanding.

Some people are born to be great, and Arthur Ashe was one of those. He couldn't be held back forever.

In 1960, he became the first African American player to win the National Junior Indoor tennis title. Three years later, he was featured in Sports Illustrated, the most popular sports magazine in America. That same year, he earned a tennis scholarship and attended the University of California, eventually graduating with a bachelor's degree in business administration. Between all of this, he made his first Davis Cup appearance, which introduced him to tennis fans all over the world.

Not satisfied with being a college graduate and a Davis Cup star, Arthur then joined the United States Army to serve his country! He quickly rose up the ranks and became known as an exemplary* soldier. His early life of discipline and hard work suited the army perfectly.

Arthur reached his first Grand Slam final while still an amateur. At the 1966 Australian Open, he lost the final (4–6, 8–6, 2–6, 3–6) to Roy Emerson. Emerson would beat him in the final the following year, too.

He had better luck at the 1968 US Open when he beat

Tom Okker in the final to lift the trophy. The match was an epic, with Arthur winning a thrilling five-set match 14–12, 5–7, 6–3, 3–6, 6–3. This was before there were tiebreaks in sets, and they went on for as long as was needed for one player to win by two clear games! This was the first of Arthur's three major titles, making him the first black men's player in history to win a Grand Slam, but he was only just getting started.

Still, Arthur faced racism every day of his life, as many people did in the 1960s. Even though he had played (and won!) his first Davis Cup in 1963, appeared in two Australian Open finals, and won the US Open, Arthur didn't officially turn professional until 1970. The people in charge of tennis had tried everything to stop him from playing at the top.

Around this time, Arthur became known around the world as a man of the people. He gave many speeches demanding equality and raised a lot of money for charity. He was almost as famous off the court as he was on it! He was adored by most tennis fans, mainly because of how amazing he was at tennis, but also because he played the game the right way. He was always fair, and he always tried to entertain.

Arthur made it third time lucky at the Australian Open finals in 1970, finally getting his hands on the trophy. He beat Dick Crealy in straight sets in one of the more dominant major final victories in history.

Arthur lost the following year's Australian Open final and then the final of the US Open in 1972, in an epic five-set battle against Ilie Năstase that could have ended with either player as champion.

His last appearance in a major final came in 1975, and it was the one that every tennis player dreamed about as a kid—Wimbledon! Arthur faced Jimmy Connors, one of the best players in the world at the time, and smashed him, 6–1, 6–1, 5–7, 6–4. He became the first black man to win Wimbledon and just the second black person ever after Althea Gibson.

Arthur retired in 1980 to concentrate on his activism*. He wrote books and traveled the world trying to help others. He suffered a heart attack at just 36 but recovered and continued to keep himself fit. But bad health ran in his family, and he passed away in 1993.

Considering all the setbacks and discrimination that he faced in his career, his achievements are nothing short of astonishing. He was the man of "firsts" and someone who will always be remembered as one of the most important players ever to pick up a racket.

THE BATTLE OF THE SEXES

Hollywood movies, documentaries, and many books have all been made about the "Battle of the Sexes." It was one of the biggest sporting events in history, yet it began more like two WWE wrestlers arguing. Billie Jean King versus Bobby Riggs was box office entertainment. It was the boys against the girls. It was feminism versus sexism*.

Billie Jean King is one of the greatest tennis players in history. She won just about everything, and her impact on women's tennis, women's rights, and LGBTQ rights was equally as significant as the work Arthur Ashe did to fight racism. She's not just an important person in the long story of tennis; she's an important person in history, full stop.

Her match against the arrogant Bobby Riggs was supposed to be an exhibition, but the heated lead-up meant it could only ever be a battle. Billie was playing for every young girl on the planet who was getting told they couldn't compete with men. Bobby Riggs was playing for fame and attention.

The woman who would go on to win 39 Grand Slams (12 in singles) was born Billie Jean Moffitt on November 22, 1943, in Long Beach, California. Her family was athletic, so sports were a huge part of her childhood. Her mother was a semi-pro swimmer, while her father played baseball and basketball and ran track. Her brother, Randy Moffitt, was a Major League Baseball pitcher. It's safe to say that sport ran in the Moffitt family!

In fact, Billie's first love was softball. According to her coaches at the time, she could also have played professionally. She made the full switch to tennis when she was 11, though, and the rest, as they say, is history!

She won her first singles major at Wimbledon in 1966 and then retained her title the following two years. She was just 22 when she started that run, and Wimbledon would become her favorite place to play. Billie won it again in 1972, 1973, and 1975, and is a 20-time champion at the All England Club* if you include doubles and mixed doubles!

Around this time, she met her future husband, TV's Larry King. She took his last name, and even when they split up years later, she kept it, as that was how people knew her by then. She would always be Billie Jean King! It was around this time that Billie was introduced to feminism, and she was instantly hooked. Women had been oppressed for far too long, and she wanted to change all of that.

Bobby Riggs had been a great player in his day. He was a former world No.1 who won several Grand Slams. But by 1973, when he was to play Billie, he was 55 and had long been retired. That meant he was out of the limelight*, which is probably why he started telling the press that the lowest-ranked men's player could beat the highest-ranked women's player. It was all done for media attention and money, but his baiting* worked. The news channels loved it, and the highest-ranked women's player at the time, Margaret Court, challenged him to a match. Riggs beat her in straight sets, and it looked like his cocky claims would be proved correct.

Margaret Court wasn't as powerful and quick as Billie Jean King, though. Billie felt that she could take Riggs. When he heard this and challenged her to a match for one hundred thousand dollars, she accepted, and the media circus began!

As the hype built, the TV channels realized that they had a global event on their hands. It seemed every country in the world wanted to show the match, and even though it was an exhibition, it ended up breaking every tennis viewing figure in history!

Bobby Riggs played up to the cameras, giving interviews where he said things about women that would see someone canceled today! Years later, he claimed that it was all an act and that he had made up with Billie, but at the time, it was shocking. Also, it seems pretty clear that a part of him believed the stuff he was saying.

As mentioned, Riggs was 55 at the time, while Billie was just 29 and in the prime of her life. She had just spent her fifth straight year at the top of the rankings, and Bobby Riggs had spent the same period partying. He rarely made time for practice, so he was out of shape, and it showed.

His match against Court earlier in the year had been

best of three, and he won in straight sets pretty easily. He had been in decent shape but had really let himself go in the months before the Battle of the Sexes. By the time he faced Billie, he looked terrible. Still, Billie was and is one of the greatest female players in history. Even if Riggs had been fitter, she probably still would have beaten him.

We must also remember that Margaret Court had just returned to tennis after giving birth. She wasn't exactly at the top of her game, either.

The Billie Jean King versus Bobby Riggs match would be the best of five, like the men's game. Billie wanted no excuses when she won. It happened on September 20, 1973, in Houston, Texas, and over 30,000 people turned up to watch. If that wasn't enough, another 90 million watched live on TV!

Riggs continued his act right up until the match began, coming out in a glittery jacket with SUGAR DADDY written on the back in shiny letters. He even kept it on through the first set to show how little he thought of his opponent. When Billie won the set 6–4, Riggs quickly checked his attitude.

Billie wasn't to be outdone, though. She decided to come out to the court surrounded by lots of ripped, shirtless men! She wanted to show the crowd and Riggs that she could have a little fun too. The only difference was that she knew when the fun needed to stop and when she had to get down to business.

Billie was much, much fitter than Riggs, and she knew it. She used this to her advantage, playing her shots deep and into the corners, forcing Riggs to move as much as possible. By the end of the first set, he was breathing hard, and his face looked like a giant beet! He even began making up excuses such as wrist cramps. He knew he was in trouble.

The second set went much the same way, with Billie easily controlling the rallies and Riggs flailing around like a fish out of water. It finished 6–3 for Billie Jean King, which would be the same score as the third set. Billie had not only beaten Riggs in straight sets but had destroyed him.

Following the match, Billie returned to the women's game as a hero. She had shown the men what women can do, and she had helped promote feminism all over the world. Bobby Riggs apologized to her in the years that followed for the way he behaved, and they later put their differences aside.

Billie Jean King often tops polls for the greatest female player of all time. She just might be, but one of her most magical moments came in an exhibition! It was the Battle of the Sexes, and it changed the way people viewed women's sports forever!

MONICA SELES'
COURAGEOUS COMEBACK

The Monica Seles incident on April 30, 1993, was one of the most shocking moments in the history of sport. It's hard to imagine that a sportsperson just doing what they do best could be approached on court by a maniac and stabbed. Things like that just don't happen.

Sadly, for Monica Seles, that nightmare was real, and she spent the rest of her career trying to move past it.

Before that awful day, Monica had experienced the type of fame that very few people ever have to deal with. She was a tennis prodigy*, and it seemed like every news channel and gossip magazine wanted a piece of her. She won eight of her nine majors while she was still a teenager, and people couldn't get enough of her.

If her career hadn't been so brutally interrupted that day, she would surely have won many more Slams.

Born on December 2, 1973, in Novi Sad, SR Serbia, Yugoslavia, Monica Seles grew up at a time in her country when things were very bad. Her family was poor, and she lived in poverty. The only escape she had was taking her old racket out onto the street to hit balls against the wall. It was here that she learned she had a special talent.

Her rise was rapid, and by the time she was 11, she was already being spoken of as the greatest prospect in the world. She won her first major, the French Open, when she was just 16, and she quickly became world news. It was the type of fame that only child actors and sporting legends such as Michael Jordan or Cristiano Ronaldo have to face. It was a terrible amount of pressure to pile onto a kid.

Monica seemed more than capable of carrying the weight, though. She won seven more Slams over the next few years, bringing her total to eight before she had even turned 20, making her the most successful teenager in the history of tennis. The early 1990s were the Monica Seles years. She was one of the rare players who continued to be loved by everyone despite winning all the time. She was adored.

Many sports writers and ex-pros believe that Monica would have gone on to be the greatest of all time if she hadn't been struck down that day. This is hard to argue with. She really was that good!

The man who would ruin her career was named Gunter Parche, a German who was obsessed with Monica's biggest opponent at the time, Steffi Graf. When Monica faced Magdalena Maleeva in the Citizen Cup in Hamburg, Germany, Parche was in the crowd. He also had a nine-inch blade hidden under his coat.

Seles had recently become world No. 1, having taken the top spot off Graf. She had just won her third French Open in a row, and it seemed like she was unstoppable.

As Monica Seles sat at a changeover during her quarterfinal match against Maleeva, Gunter Parche casually walked onto the court, approached her, and sank his knife into her back. For a moment, everyone watching didn't react. It just seemed like a fan had walked up to a player and tapped her on the shoulder or something.

Then they saw the blood.

What followed was horrible, as stewards and security ran to help. Monica was in shock and bleeding out, and her world had just been turned upside down.

Several things happened in the following years that upset Monica Seles. First of all, the man who stabbed her didn't go to prison. He got off with a slap on the wrist*. Secondly, the tennis board decided that the tournament should continue, which felt like an insult to everything Monica had gone through. From that moment on, she lost faith in professional tennis. She knew the players meant nothing to the people who ran it. It was all about the money to them.

Monica Seles missed two years while she recovered. The physical damage eventually healed, but the mental wounds would scar her forever. How could they not?

Every time she stepped onto a tennis court, she had to remember what had happened to her. Whenever she sat down between sets and looked at the crowd, she must have seen the face of the man who attacked her. If a ball boy or ball girl came up behind her with a towel, Monica would have held her breath.

Somehow, she still managed to compete again, and not just in the smaller tournaments. Monica Seles reached four more Grand Slam finals! She lost two of them to Steffi Graf, which must have hurt, seeing as the man who stabbed her claimed he did it to get Graf back to world No. 1. Would a fully fit and clear-headed Seles have beaten Graf? Probably. She had beaten her in several finals before Parche's horrific attack.

Between those two Graf losses, Seles met German player Anke Huber in the 1996 Australian Open final. Seles destroyed her 6–4, 6–1 to win her first and only major since her return. One more Slam final came two years later at the French Open, but she lost a close match to Arantxa Sánchez Vicario.

To come back from something as awful as being stabbed in the middle of a tennis match surrounded by thousands of people would destroy most people, but Monica Seles isn't most people! She came through poverty and pain as a kid, which hardened her against the cruelties of the world. And even though she has been hardened, she remains one of the nicest people in sports.

That's her true strength. She's been able to live her life in kindness and joy despite the horrors she's been forced to face.

VENUS & SERENA: TRAILBLAZERS

Venus and Serena Williams blew through tennis like a hurricane. They were like nothing ever seen before, with their power and speed helping them become the most dominant force in tennis. But it never could have happened if they hadn't been so determined. They came through some awful times to reach the top, and that's what makes their story so amazing.

They were born a year apart (Venus is one year older) in Compton, California, in a neighborhood known more for crime and murder than tennis. In fact, finding a tennis court in the area was nearly impossible. It was seen as a rich person's sport and not the type of thing for two black girls from the streets of Compton.

Even decades after the hard work of legends such as Arthur Ashe, who did so much for equality in tennis, it was still seen as a mostly white sport. Venus and Serena changed all of that.

Their father, Richard, was very strict. He made the kids train super hard, and he never let them think they wouldn't make it. He had no background in tennis, yet he trained them like he was an ex-pro. He had one vision—that both of his daughters would become professional tennis stars. It was far too much pressure to put on children, but the two girls somehow handled it.

The sisters practiced with second-hand rackets, tattered balls, and homemade equipment, usually on the street instead of on courts. Seeing that his girls wouldn't get to use proper courts much, Richard insisted on extra strength and fitness training instead. The girls ran every morning and lifted weights. This would help mold them into the powerful players they would become years later.

Unlike Arthur Ashe, the girls were allowed to enter any youth tournament they wished. The only problem was that many of them were very expensive, so Richard and his wife had to use their savings. Again, this put huge pressure on the girls to succeed. Even at 10 and 11, they knew that if they didn't win whatever tournament they were in, the family might go hungry. Luckily, they won pretty much every tournament they entered, especially when they played doubles!

As soon as they entered the pro tour, they dominated. Venus reached her first major final at just 17, losing to Martina Hingis in the final of the US Open. She became the first African American woman since 1958 to do so.

Two years later, Serena matched her sister, reaching the US Open final in 1999. She was also 17, and she won! It was the first of her 23 Slams.

By 2002, Venus was ranked No. 1 and Serena No. 2. They were so dominant some people believed nobody else would win anything as long as the girls were around. Of course, this was a bit of an exaggeration, but it really did feel that way.

With both sisters being so good, it also meant they met each other quite often in tournaments and usually in the final. They had an intense rivalry, but they never fell out. Between 2001 and 2017, they faced each other in nine Slam finals! Four of those finals came in the space of one year. Between the 2002 French Open and the 2003 Australian Open, they played each other in four major finals in a row, with Serena winning them all as she seemed to move to a different level.

But it was Wimbledon where the sisters really dominated. Between 2000 and 2016, they won 12 of the 17 tournaments between them! Venus won five, while Serena won slightly more with seven.

Throughout all of this, they basically owned doubles. Whenever they entered a doubles tournament, they were expected to win, and they usually did. By 2001, they had won a Career Golden Slam* in doubles, having won their first gold in doubles at the Olympic Games in 2000. Venus also won the singles gold that year, something Serena would also do in 2012. They won doubles gold again in 2008 and 2012.

At the time of that Golden Slam, Venus was just 20, and Serena was 19. They had already conquered the world of tennis.

Venus and Serena Williams grew up in a neighborhood where dreams of making it in tennis were just that—dreams. The idea that one of them, never mind two, could grow up to dominate the world of tennis was seen as impossible. But as you will see throughout this book, there is no such thing as impossible in sports. The people who make it to the top are always special, which helps them do special things!

Serena Williams is now seen as the greatest female player of all time. Venus is certainly in the top 15. Together, they are possibly the most dominant siblings* in the history of any sport. Their stacked trophy cabinet is all the proof we need!

THE MAGIC LIFE OF MANSOUR BAHRAMI

Some of you may have heard of Mansour Bahrami, and to some of you, he may be a completely new name. Those of you who have heard of him will almost certainly know of him as the trick-shot guy who has entertained fans for decades with his legendary through-the-legs shots and on-court jokes.

But what very few people know about Bahrami is the incredible and unlikely journey he had to take even to become a tennis player. Yes, he might not have won a major like many of the others in this book, but that doesn't make his story any less amazing. Mansour had to overcome war, poverty and even using a frying pan as a racket to reach his dream of becoming a pro. If that's not inspiring, then I don't know what is!

Mansour Bahrami was born in Arak, Iran, on April 26, 1956. At the time, Iran was a nation where tennis wasn't even played. It was seen as a Western* sport, and that was considered evil. Mansour used to read about the tennis stars of the time in old magazines and paper clippings. He adored the idea of it, and he dreamed of one day becoming a pro.

His parents demanded he give up any such dream, but he wouldn't listen. He used to slip away and practice with an old frying pan, hitting bundled-up, taped rags against a wall. As he reached his teens, Iran collapsed into civil war. The new Islamic rule meant that tennis wasn't just ignored; it was now against the law to play. Mansour had to be more careful than ever.

He had to sneak away to play in the Davis Cup when he was 16, but his team was made up of players with little to no experience in tennis, and they lost heavily. Still, Mansour's talents shone through, and he found that he could compete with the best players in the world. He made it his mission to escape Iran and chase his dream.

With what little savings he had, Mansour packed his bags and made for the border, working his way to France. In his backpack, he had nothing more than a few sets of clothes and his favorite thing in the world— his tennis racket. It was a step up from using a frying pan, but still a long way from the luxuries that all the other pros in the world had.

He hadn't gotten his first racket until the age of 13, and this was still the same one. Mansour was a man now, having been forced to stay in Iran throughout his teens and early 20s. Even though he had missed out on his prime years as a player, he never gave up his dream of stepping out onto the court surrounded by tennis fans.

Things didn't instantly change when he finally got to France. He had no money, and he often had to sleep rough. He barely ate, and any money he did have was spent on entry fees for local tennis tournaments. If he didn't get far in the events, he would lose his money. If he won, he would have some money for a while, but it never lasted long. He was literally playing for his dinner.

After his visa* ran out, he was forced to live as an illegal immigrant. He had to constantly hide from the police to avoid being deported. All of this, added to his lack of food and shelter, meant his fitness suffered. It was something he would never fully recover from, and it meant that he was always behind his opponents on the pro tour.

Mansour found he could do much better in doubles. He had all the talent in the world, but he used to burn out in long singles matches. In doubles, he could reserve some of his energy and share the physical load with his partner. This way, Mansour was able to stay sharp until the very end of matches, and when that happened, very few could stand a chance.

Around this time, he also discovered he was a born entertainer. He loved showing off for the crowd, and they adored him for it. He always played with a smile on his face, and his trick shots were like nothing ever seen before. In his later years, Mansour would make a good living playing exhibition matches, where he could interact with the fans and show off his out-of-this-world tricks and charisma.

You see, Mansour didn't play his first professional match until he was in his 30s! He was an illegal immigrant, so he couldn't get on the pro tour until he had French citizenship*. He had spent over a decade bouncing between cheap apartments and sleeping on the street, never having enough food or training. To come from that and still make it to the pro tour is a miracle.

Alongside his doubles partner, Eric Winogradsky, the

pair won two doubles tournaments and reached the final of the French Open in 1989. It all came a little too late for Mansour, who was pretty much past his prime by the time he made it. He had come too far to just quit, though, and he found his home on the senior's tour.

He not only became a star of the senior's tour, but he became the man that everyone wanted to see. There could be legends such as McEnroe and Connors playing before, but if Bahrami's name was on the list for the doubles, that's what would really fill the stadiums. His through-the-legs-shots (hotdogs), kneeling shots, behind-the-back shots, and so many more became legendary across the world, and his pure happiness and joy to be there was infectious!

Mansour Bahrami could have given up on his dream so many times, yet he refused. Even when he reached France, there seemed to be no way for him to make it. Again, he stood tall, and he tried and tried until he reached the top. He knew what he wanted, and he refused to give up.

Despite a childhood of living in war and suffering, Mansour continues to spend his life making others smile. He is a born entertainer and one of those special people who make the world a better place just by being themselves. He is a true legend of the game, but not in the way we might think. There might not be a bunch of trophies on his mantle, but to many fans, he will never be forgotten.

NOVAK DJOKOVIC'S UNBREAKABLE WILL

We all know Novak Djokovic as one of the most legendary winners in tennis. He is the only man to complete a Career Golden Masters*, and at the time this book was written, he had won 99 singles titles! Twenty-four of them were Grand Slams, and to top it off, he is an Olympic gold medalist.

But things didn't start off easily for Novak. Like many people on this list, he had to come through hard times to reach the top. And they weren't just hard times— they were horrific.

Novak Djokovic grew up in Belgrade, SR Serbia, SFR Yugoslavia, which is now Serbia. He was born in 1987, right around the time that the civil war broke out. It was the Yugoslav Wars, and it was brutal. As a child, Novak would hear gunfire every day, and he walked to school surrounded by crumbling buildings and bomb damage.

At home, he was surrounded by sports. His father, Srdjan, was a professional skier, while his two brothers ended up having careers in tennis too. They were never as good as Novak, but who is?

Novak began playing tennis at age 4 when his father gave him a plastic racket and foam ball. Srdjan later claimed that for the next few years, he never saw Novak without his racket and ball. He took it everywhere. His new hobby was a way of pretending his country wasn't being torn apart by war, and it gave him an escape.

By the time Novak was 6, his talent was there for all to see. Sadly, he couldn't practice properly, as any courts in Belgrade were either destroyed or being used as storage for the war. His father used every penny he had to send his son to a training camp outside the city. He did this to help Novak with his career and to keep him safe.

While at the training camp, Novak met former Yugoslav professional player Jelena Gencic. Gencic saw real talent in Novak and got to work helping him improve his game. Novak's hero was legendary American player Pete Sampras, who was huge at the time. So far, he had based his whole game on Sampras', but Gencic taught him to create his own style. She told him to hit a double-handed backhand as it suited his game more. Novak listened, and he was soon on his way to being the best junior player in Europe.

He trained with Gencic for six years, and by the time he left the camp, he felt ready to take the next step. Unfortunately, the war was still raging, so he had no way of keeping up his training. Novak was forced to practice in empty, abandoned swimming pools just so he couldn't be seen by the bombers flying overhead.

He later told interviewers that he woke up most nights screaming as the sound of bombs being dropped shook the whole family out of bed. Sirens went off all the time, and when they did, every student had to hide under their desks until they stopped. The school could only open some days, and when it did, Novak would walk there with his brothers, often stepping past bodies in the street. It was a terrible way for a child to live and we are all eternally grateful that Novak was able to survive it unscathed.

As he got older, his father knew Novak needed to leave Belgrade if he was to become a pro. He took out many loans to fund his son and sent him on his way. Novak knew that his father's sacrifice would have been for nothing if he didn't make it in tennis, and the family would be broke.

Years later, as he was winning Slams like they were nothing, he explained how he deals with pressure so well. He pointed out that playing in a final was nothing compared to the pressure of destroying your family if you don't make it. Playing in a Slam final was a dream, not a nightmare, so how could he not enjoy himself?

Novak used the money his father borrowed to travel to Germany, where he met coach Nikola Pilic, who ran an academy in Oberschleissheim. Novak was just 12, but he had the maturity of an adult. He'd been through so much. He spent several years there perfecting his game before he felt he was ready for the pro tour.

He traveled around Germany playing amateur tournaments. Then he moved on to France and finally America. He was quickly earning a reputation as one of the best young players in the world, and people spoke of his calm determination and incredible game. He won his first major in 2008, the Australian Open, an event he would dominate throughout his career. So far, as of 2024, he's won it 10 times!

That Australian Open victory also stopped the Nadal-Federer dominance that had seen the two players share the previous 11 Slams. He butted his way in, and the dominant two soon became known as the Big Three. Between them, they created a golden era, and tennis fans know there will probably never be a time again when three all-time greats compete against each other in their prime.

Even in his late thirties in 2024, Novak continues to be at the very top of the game. He has always kept himself insanely fit, and his hunger to win seems to increase with every trophy. Who knows how long he can stay at the top, but if anyone deserves it, it's him. To come through war, death, and then being separated from your family for most of your childhood takes a certain type of person. It takes a hero.

Novak Djokovic has also become an entertainer. His exhibition matches are always the hottest ticket in town, and they always show a side of him that is sometimes hidden when he is trying to win majors. The serious, win-at-all-costs Novak takes a back seat, and the funny, caring entertainer shows up. That shows real class, something that has helped Novak become one of the most successful sportspeople in the world.

COCO GAUFF
TOPPLES THE QUEEN

Every young superstar has to get old one day. When they do, there is usually a new kid on the block who wants to take their place. That's the circle of life! However, when Coco Gauff burst onto the scene and beat her hero, Venus Williams, it was a real shock. Why? Because Coco Gauff was just 15!

While growing up, Venus and Serena Williams meant everything to Coco Gauff. Her dream was to one day play against them, but she never could have imagined it would happen so soon. In fact, given the age difference, she probably didn't expect it to happen at all. Surely the Williams sisters would be retired by the time Coco was old enough to play them?

If Coco had been a regular player, that might be true. But she is so good that she was qualifying for the main draw in Slams as young as 15, which made her the youngest player in the Open Era to do so.

Coco Gauff was born on March 13, 2004, in Atlanta, Georgia. At the time of this book being written, she is still only 20, yet she has won nine Women's Tennis Association (WTA) Tour singles titles, including one major at the US Open. She also has nine doubles titles, including the French Open!

Coco's father was a college basketball star, while her

mother was a track and field athlete at Florida State University. Coco's two younger brothers were also very good at sports. Growing up, she learned how to compete and how to stay humble.

Her first taste of tennis came when she was 6, and within a year, her family could see she had a special talent. To help her develop, they moved to Delray Beach, where there were better academies. Both of her parents gave up their careers to concentrate on Coco's tennis. Her mother homeschooled her, and her father trained her.

By age 10, Coco was already considered one of America's most promising athletes. She moved to France for a while to attend the Mouratoglou Tennis Academy, which was run by the legendary coach Patrick Mouratoglou. This was brilliant for Coco, as Mouratoglou had been Serena Williams' coach for a long time, as well as many other of the greats. After seeing Coco play, her new coach claimed he had never seen such athleticism and determination in such a young player.

Coco dominated as a junior and quickly became world No. 1. She made her junior Grand Slam debut at the Australian Open in 2017, making it all the way to the final despite only being 13 years old. She went one better the following year, when she won the Junior French Open at 14 years old, and it was clear that she wasn't only going to be a star, she could go on to be one of the greatest players in history.

Despite her scarily young age, by the time 2019 came around, it was clear that she was ready to move up to the professional levels of tennis. She adjusted incredibly well to life on the WTA Tour, winning multiple main draw matches, but had failed to get past the second round of qualifying at the first two Grand Slams of the year. However, this was all about to change.

She was 15 years and 3 months old at the 2019 Wimbledon Championships, and yet she started off like a seasoned pro. In qualifying, she beat Aliona Bolsova and Greet Minnen to become the youngest player in the Open Era to qualify for the main draw. And if that wasn't amazing enough for her, Coco was then drawn against her idol, Venus Williams!

Coco could have been forgiven for being a little starstruck*. She was stepping out onto the court in front of millions of TV viewers, and she was face-to-face with her hero. Venus was still one of the best around and, with all her experience behind her, was expected to beat her teenage opponent easily. But as we know, that's not the way it played out at all!

Coco beat Venus Williams 6-4 6-4 to shock everyone watching. It was clear that at that moment, a star was born. Coco had stepped out onto one of the biggest courts in the world at her first Grand Slam against her childhood idol and had won. If it were a movie, you would say it is too unbelievable to be true!

The Coco Gauff fairy tale didn't end there. She then beat Magdalena Rybarikova in the second round. After that, she beat world No. 60 Polona Hercog in an epic match that saw Coco save two match points on her way to victory. Not only had the fans now seen how talented she was, but they had also witnessed her fighting spirit. It was insane that a 15-year-old kid could have so much guts.

To make the dream even more amazing, that match against Hercog was played on Centre Court, the most magical court on the planet. No tennis court holds that much history. It's the dream of every player to one day step onto the grass at Centre Court, and Coco did it at 15!

She was back there again for her fourth-round match, as the Wimbledon organizers quickly realized that Coco was box office. Everyone wanted to see her play. Sadly, the fourth round was a step too far for such a young kid, and she lost to an in-form Simona Halep. Halep would go on to win the title, so there was no shame in losing to her, and Coco put up a good fight.

Coco's fourth-round match was the most-watched of any on ESPN of the tournament, meaning that more people watched it than the final! Her performance at Wimbledon also shot her up the rankings, which meant that it wasn't long before she could get straight into the main draw of all the other majors.

Of course, Coco didn't stop there. She continued to improve with every tournament and, after steadily rising up the women's game, made her first major final at the 2022 French Open. She came up against an inspired Iga Świątek, who proved too good on the day, but everyone watching knew it was only a matter of time before Coco was a major champion.

That victory came the following year when she beat

the amazing Aryna Sabalenka in the final of the US Open. Again, Coco showed her fighting spirit, coming back to win after dropping the first set. The match finished 2–6, 6–3, 6–2, and the victory made her the first American teenager to win the US Open since Serena Williams.

Coco Gauff is not only a born champion, but she is also a wonderful person. In 2024, at just 20, she has already done more charity work than most celebrities do in their lifetime. When she was 19, she helped pay for the construction of tennis courts in East Atlanta's Brownwood Park so that kids would have a place to go play.

How many Slams will Coco win during her career? Who knows? But the sky is the limit!

FAIRYTALE
RUNS

EMMA RADUCANU:
FROM QUALIFIER TO CHAMPION

Fairy-tale runs in sports are always amazing. To see someone who wasn't expected to win or a player coming back from tragedy to lift the title is a beautiful sight. It gives everyone hope. All the stories in this section are inspirational, and none more so than Emma Raducanu's unbelievable US Open victory in 2021.

When Emma Raducanu won the US Open at just 18, she became hugely famous overnight. She also became the first British woman to win a Grand Slam since Virginia Wade in 1977. Being so young was just one of the reasons that the news channels and magazines wanted a piece of her. Emma is a beautiful and stylish girl, which can sometimes make a career in sports harder than it should be.

That might sound strange, but Emma was instantly hounded* by the press. She couldn't go anywhere without photographers snapping her picture or someone shoving a microphone in her face. All she's ever wanted to do is play tennis, and these people were always getting in the way of that.

But we're here to talk about her fairy-tale US Open victory, which happened while she was still an unknown teenager dreaming of one day reaching the top!

Emma Raducanu was born in Toronto, Ontario, Canada, on November 12, 2002. She didn't live there for long and pretty much spent her whole childhood in Bromley, England. She considers herself English.

Her father is Romanian, and her mother is from China, so she has always been surrounded by wonderful different cultures. Both of her parents are academics*, which meant Emma grew up in a home where study was very important. She learned Romanian from her father, Chinese from her mother, and English at school. She is fluent in all three languages!

She first played tennis at age 5, but she also loved soccer, basketball, motocross, go-karting, and ballet! While attending Bickley Primary School, her teachers claimed she was one of the smartest students in her year. Some people just seem to have all the talent, huh!

Emma played her first International Tennis Federation (ITF) junior match the day she turned 13, which is the minimum age allowed to enter. She couldn't wait any longer! Amazingly, she won the tournament, which was actually an under-18 event. It made her the youngest player in history to win one.

She turned pro in 2018 when she was just 15. Her coaches knew she could compete at that level, but Emma was still developing. The adults would always have more power than her. They made her rotate between senior and junior tournaments for a couple of years to keep her game sharp and prevent her from burning out like so many teenage sensations in the past have done.

Just as her professional career was taking off, the COVID-19 pandemic hit. All tournaments were canceled for a while, and only a few could be played when things started up again. To keep her fitness up, she played exhibition matches and small local events.

By early 2021, she was still basically unknown. When she made her WTA Tour main draw debut at the Nottingham Open, Emma felt like she had a chance. A first-round defeat to fellow British player Harriet Dart brought Emma back down to earth. It was a wake-up call, and she used it to her advantage.

Sometimes, things that seem bad can happen in our lives, and maybe they are at the time, but we can learn from them and help ourselves move forward. Emma used her defeat as a warning. It let her know that the pro players were a whole lot better than anything she had faced before. Even the lower-ranked pros were a step up. Emma knuckled down and practiced twice as hard.

Not long after that Nottingham Open loss, she had her big break. It wasn't the US Open—that would come soon after—but Wimbledon. The big one for any British player out there.

Emma put on a real show in front of the adoring British crowd, who always love to see a home-grown player challenging for the title. She was given a wild card into the main draw and made full use of the opportunity. She beat Vitalia Diatchenko in the first round, beat the future Wimbledon champion Markéta Vondroušová in the second round, and then beat tennis veteran Sorana Cîrstea in the third round. Not only had she stunned the world by making it so far, but she did so without dropping a set!

Emma didn't lose her round of 16 match but had to retire in the second set with breathing problems. Little did she know that it was the first of many physical problems she would suffer throughout her short career. Something else that would happen regularly in her career occurred around that time, too. Emma changed her coach, which she has done many times since.

The coaching change seemed strange at the time, but in hindsight, it was a stroke of genius. Andrew Richardson became her coach a few weeks before the US Open, and he watched as she stunned the tennis world in one of the most dominant performances the US Open has ever seen.

Emma began the US Open like a steam train, winning her three qualifying matches in straight sets. Her closest match came in the second round of qualifying, where she won 6-3 7-5, and unbelievably, this was the closest match that she had all tournament!

She carried on the main draw where she left off, defying the odds to demolish anyone who stepped onto the court with her. She brushed aside Stefanie Vögele, Zhang Shuai, Sara Sorribes Tormo, and Shelby Rogers on the way to the quarterfinals, making them look like amateur club players rather than elite pros. She came up against her first world-class player in the last eight, world number 11 Belinda Bencic, but once again, showed that she was on another level by winning 6-3 6-4.

By reaching the semifinals, she became only the fifth qualifier to do so in the Open Era, but the fairytale run was not over there. With the world willing her on, she then beat world number 17 Maria Sakkari 6-1 6-4, meaning that in just her second Grand Slam main draw appearance, she had made it to the final. Not only this, but her win shot her up to number 23 in the world and catapulted her to the British number one spot!

Just like with Raducanu, another player had been having a fairytale run at the 2021 US Open. She faced Canadian teenager Leylah Fernandez in the final, who had also defied the odds to make it to the championship match, and whose run to the final could well be in a book like this. It made for the first all-teenage Grand Slam final since 1999, and everyone knew that history would be made with either winner.

Emma had been unstoppable in every round, but she was just a kid, really. Pressure can do funny things to people, and sometimes they crumble at the last moment when it gets too much. Not Emma. She played the final like it was nothing!

Much like every other round, Emma played sensational tennis to win in straight sets. She beat Fernandez 6–4, 6–3, smashing a 109-mile-per-hour ace to win on match point! It was the perfect way to claim the victory and summed up an absolutely ridiculous tournament from the young Brit. Not only had she become Britain's first women's Grand Slam champion since 1977, but she was also the first qualifier, in men's or women's tennis, to win a major in the Open Era. And she did all this without dropping a set! It is undoubtedly one of the most incredibly and unlikely Grand Slam runs tennis has ever seen, and it will live on forever in tennis history.

Sadly, Emma struggled to cope with the fame and expectation after this remarkable win, and was not helped by the many injuries and illnesses that seemed to put her back every time she was building some momentum again. But the past year has been very positive for her and she seems to be returning back to that legendary form of 2021. As this book is being written, she has returned to the top 60 in the world and only seems to be heading up from there. Will she win another major? Only time will tell. Even if she doesn't, her fairytale win at the 2021 will forever cement her spot as a legend of the sport.

THE WILDCARD WHO WON
WIMBLEDON

Goran Ivanisevic was a fan's favorite. He was one of those players who could travel to any country and play in any tournament, and most of the crowd would cheer for him. He had passion, charm, and one of the most powerful serves the world has ever seen. Seriously, the guy's serve was so big that it should have been registered as a lethal weapon!

Goran had an incredibly successful career and is undoubtedly a tennis great. He won 22 ATP titles, reached a career-high ranking of number two in the world, and consistently reached the final stages of Grand Slams. However, for a long time, it seemed that he was going to be one of those great players who could never quite get over the line in the final of a major, which was an achievement that his game definitely deserved.

This was, of course, until his fairytale run at Wimbledon in 2001, where he etched his name in the history books forever...

Goran Ivanisevic was born in Split, SR Croatia, Yugoslavia, on September 13, 1971. His talent for tennis showed early, and he quickly learned that he had an especially powerful serve. Goran was tall for his age, and he used this to his advantage. His height meant that he was able to slam the ball from a higher angle, not only giving him more power than his fellow players, but also meaning that he could reach a much larger area of the service box and hit crazy angles out wide and down the tee.

He was lucky enough to be spotted by legendary coach Jelena Gencic. Jelena would earn the reputation as one of the greatest coaches of all time, with her students going on to win 36 Slams between them! Some of the players she coached include Monica Seles and Novak Djokovic!

Goran turned pro in 1988 and instantly won a doubles title in Frankfurt, Germany, with his playing partner, Rudiger Haas. Although he would have a successful doubles career, Goran always saw himself as a singles player. He felt he was good enough to win a major on his own. It just took him a little longer than he expected!

Soon after turning pro, he caused a shock at the Australian Open when he reached the quarterfinals as a qualifier. News of his rocket serve quickly spread, but some people questioned whether he had strong enough groundstrokes to back it up. This was something he'd have to hear throughout his career.

At the French Open the following year, he showed what he could do when he knocked out the legendary Boris Becker. Once more, he reached the quarterfinals but fell short.

His brilliant start to his career continued, and he reached the semifinals at Wimbledon, the tournament where he would become the most loved by the fans.

The British crowd adored him, so it was fitting that he won his one and only Slam there years later.

Goran finished 1990 with his first singles title in Stuttgart, Germany, before winning the World Team Cup with Yugoslavia*.

In 1992, he reached his first Slam final, once more at Wimbledon. In fact, of the four Slam finals he reached, all of them were at Wimbledon. His run at that year's event was epic, and he knocked out some greats, including Pete Sampras and Boris Becker (again). Against Sampras in the semis, one of the greatest players in history and a future seven-time Wimbledon champion, Goran served 36 aces and didn't face a break point once!

The final against another fan favorite, Andre Agassi, was a classic. Both players were looking to win their first major, and they came at each other with everything they had. The match was a back-and-forth war, with both players sharing the first four sets. Agassi eventually got over the line, 6-4 in the fifth, and Goran was devastated. Still, he picked himself up and finished the summer by winning bronze at the 1992 Olympic Games!

He reached the final of Wimbledon again in 1994, but he lost in straight sets to Pete Sampras. Goran finished the year with his highest-ever ranking of 2nd in the world, but he still couldn't win that first Slam. Questions about his game from the back of the court continued to be asked.

By 1998, Goran still hadn't won a Slam. Everyone

believed his chance had come and gone. He reached the Wimbledon final again that year, and once more, he came up against Pete Sampras. Pistol Pete was almost unstoppable on the grass at this point, and despite another heroic effort, where he took him to five sets, ended with another close loss in a major final for Goran. The pain on his face after the match was impossible to miss. He looked broken.

The next few years for Goran were devastating. He suffered a serious shoulder injury that threatened to destroy his once unbreakable serve. With his strongest weapon gone, he slid down the rankings. By 2001, he was 125th in the world. In fact, he even needed a wild card just to get into his favorite tournament, Wimbledon, that year, and unlike previous years, nothing was expected of him.

The once crowd-favorite had to play his first few rounds on the outside courts, which would have been an insult to the big-serving Croat a few years before, but now he was just fortunate to be playing at the tournament. Despite his shoulder preventing his serve from being as devastating as it usually was, Goran started moving through the draw with relative ease, to the surprise of everyone watching. Helped by some of the best returning of his life, he beat Carlos Moya, Andy Roddick, Greg Rusedski and Marat Safin, and before anyone knew it, he was in the semifinals again.

His semifinal against the home favorite Tim Henman was unreal. It is still considered one of the greatest battles ever seen at Wimbledon and could have easily made the Greatest Matches section in this book. An epic back-and-forth clash saw Goran come from the dead several times, pulling off miracle shots when it seemed like he had nothing left. In the end, he won the match 7-5 6-7 0-6 7-6 6-3 over three days of playing, and both players were given a standing ovation as they left the court.

Goran should have been too exhausted to put up a fight in the final against the Australian Pat Rafter, but he somehow found the strength to compete. Another epic unfolded, and the match lasted over three hours. It finished 6–3, 3–6, 6–3, 2–6, 9–7 in favor of Goran in another Wimbledon epic. It was literally a punch-for-punch war!

The delight on Goran's face as he lifted the famous trophy will forever remain one of Wimbledon's most special images. He had finally gotten his hands on that major trophy that he so desperately deserved, and even better, it was at the major that mattered most to him - Wimbledon. This made him not only the lowest-ranked men's player to win Wimbledon in history but also the first wild card. Everyone watching in the stadium and on TV shared his joy. It was one of those moments that just felt special.

MICHAEL CHANG'S
MIRACLE RUN IN PARIS

The story of Michael Chang is kind of the opposite of Goran Ivanisevic's comeback from nowhere. Ivanisevic won his one and only major right at the end of his career, whereas Michael Chang won his one very early and then never won one again!

Another thing that separates Chang and Ivanisevic is height. Goran was very tall, which helped him develop his dominating serve. Michael Chang was always small for a tennis player at 5 feet 9 inches, so he had to rely heavily on his speed, groundstrokes, and defensive game.

Michael Chang was born in Hoboken, New Jersey, on February 22, 1972. His parents had recently emigrated from Taiwan, and after a couple of years in Hoboken, the family moved to St. Paul, Minnesota. This was where Michael first discovered tennis. He loved it from the moment he first held a racket.

After seeing that their son had a real talent, his parents decided to move again, this time to California. They felt Michael had the best chance of progressing in California, as there were many more academies and opportunities for kids. His mother even quit her job as a chemist so she could travel around the country with him for junior tournaments.

Despite his size, Michael quickly earned a reputation as one of the best young players in America. By the age of 12, he had already set multiple junior records and won his first national title. Just one year later, he won the under-16s at the Fiesta Bowl, and in one United States Tennis Association Junior Hard Court singles tournament, he even beat a young Pete Sampras in the final!

It was pretty clear that Michael couldn't be held back for much longer, and he made the jump to professional tennis at just 15. He became the youngest men's player to win a main draw match at the US Open when he beat Paul McNamee in four sets. A month later, he broke another record when he reached the semifinal in Scottsdale, Arizona, making him the youngest men's player ever to reach the semis of a pro tournament.

If getting to a semifinal at 15 was impressive, he topped it when he won a pro tournament at 16!

Michael spent his early career breaking many "youngest-ever" records. Of course, the record-breaking French Open victory was yet to come, but it wasn't far away! It came at Roland-Garros (another name for the French Open) at the start of the summer in 1989, and it was special!

Although the final was a classic, his fourth-round win over world No. 1 Ivan Lendl is remembered as perhaps the best of the tournament. Lendl was not only the world No. 1, but he had also won the French Open three times already. Lendl had been an almost unbeatable force on the French clay, and he was expected to win quite easily. He was playing a teenager, after all!

Michael Chang might have been 17, but he was electric and played with the knowledge and strength of a player ten years his senior. Still, he might have felt he had bitten off more than he could chew when Lendl won the first two sets and went a break up in the third. To make matters worse, Michael nearly had to retire with leg cramps. They were so bad he could barely run. He shook them off as best he could as he mounted the comeback to end all comebacks!

Because of his cramps, Michael had to change his game. He began taking more and more risks, as he needed the rallies to end as quickly as possible so that he didn't have to run as much. Up until this point, Michael's game had been that of a counter-puncher*, but he somehow defied all logic to produce some of the most devastating and attacking tennis we have ever seen. Despite at times running on just one leg, he came roaring back to win the final three sets, all with a score of 6-3, to come back from the dead against the world number one.

He then beat Ronald Agenor and Andrei Chesnokov to get to the final, where he would face one of the best players in the world at the time, Stefan Edberg.

The final was another classic, and after the four-hour and 37-minute match against Ivan Lendl less than a week before, the last thing Chang needed was another long match. But that's what he got! The final against Edberg was like a heavyweight boxing match, with both players trading blows.

The first set was pretty one-sided, and Chang won it 6–1. Edberg stormed back, winning the next two sets 6-3 6-4. It looked like Chang's exhaustion and his lack of experience would catch up to him, but his fighting spirit shone through. He won the fourth set 6–4 to bring the final to a decider.

By that point, it was Edberg who looked more tired. It was clear that Chang's tenacious counter-punching style was getting to him, and it started to look like he was running out of answers. The little 17-year-old seemed to be full of energy all of a sudden, and his speed around the court was stunning. He somehow managed to return, dig out, and scramble everything Edberg threw at him and must have looked more like a brick wall to Edberg than a teenager.

Michael Chang won the last set 6–2 and was the French Open champion. He became very emotional on the court, and it was later revealed that he had been dealing with a lot of personal stuff. Literally, at that moment, the Tiananmen Square Massacre* was taking place, and Michael had been thinking of his mother's homeland and all the tragedy that was happening.

He hadn't even trained in the days before the final, as he'd been glued to the TV with his family leading up to it. They had been watching the news nonstop for any updates of the horrors taking place in China.

Michael's victory made him the first American to win the French Open since 1955 and the first to win a Slam since 1984. It began a new era of success in American tennis as players such as Pete Sampras and Andre Agassi also burst onto the scene. None of them would win a major at such a young age, though. Michael's win made him the youngest men's player in history to win a major (which he still holds) and the youngest player in history to get into the top 5!

Michael reached the final of a few more Slams but never won another. His highest ranking was No. 2, and he won 34 ATP Tour titles. It was a very successful career, but probably not as amazing as it could have been. Still, he will always be remembered for that fantastic French Open when he played two of the greatest matches ever seen on his way to winning the title at just 17 years and 109 days old!

KIM CLIJSTERS
PUTS FAMILY FIRST

When Kim Clijsters first appeared on our TV, she was seen as the great Belgian hope. Tennis wasn't really that popular in Belgium at the time, so when she burst onto the scene with another great player, Justine Henin, the Belgian people suddenly had two top players to cheer for. They were like buses: You wait ages for one to show up, and then all of a sudden, two come along at once!

Unfortunately for Kim and Justine, they broke through just as Venus and Serena Williams were starting their careers. So, for Kim Clijsters to win four majors in her career, she had to be fantastic. She also managed to reach world No. 1 in both singles and doubles. That's why it came as such a shock when she retired at just 23.

Kim wanted to start a family, and she felt that being on tour all the time wasn't the best way to raise kids. She stepped away from the sport and began a new life as a wife and mother.

The call of tennis was strong, though, and Kim knew that one day she'd have to return. After a few years away, she began training again. Kim knew she would return as an unranked player, so she would have to start at the bottom again. Also, she wouldn't be able to play in as many tournaments as she would like, as she still wanted to spend quality time with her family.

What makes her story so special is that she won three of her four Slams after returning from her retirement. Giving birth takes a lot out of women, and to come back to any sport afterward shows incredible strength and determination. When she told the press that she was coming out of retirement, a lot of people wondered if she could ever reach the heights she once had. Kim would prove them all wrong!

After just three warmup tournaments, she entered the US Open, a tournament she had won once before her early retirement. She was unranked and pretty much dismissed.

After receiving a wild card into the main draw of the 2009 US Open, Kim began showing the type of form that had made her one of the best young players in the world. Still, when she came up against Serena Williams in the semifinals, it was seen as a step too far. Serena was the defending champion and in the form of her life.

The match was brilliant, with all the drama of two GOATS butting heads! Kim took the first set 6–4 before the end of the second set erupted. A foot-fault* was called on Serena, who was serving at 6-5 down in the second set, which gave Clijsters two match points. Serena couldn't believe that the call had been made on such an important point, and this, coupled with the fact that she was certain she never foot-faulted caused her to argue more than she should have with the umpire and line judge. In one of the more controversial moments in tennis history, Serena was given a point penalty, meaning that Clijsters automatically won the match.

She then faced Danish player Caroline Wozniacki, who would later go on to spend 71 weeks ranked No. 1 in the world, but at this point, was still an up-and-coming player in her first major final. Both women had a similar game, but that only meant it would be a closely fought battle and would make for some excellent rallies.

Kim won the first set 7–5, with each player showing their amazing all-court* skills. Losing the set after such a battle seemed to drain Wozniacki, who tried her best in the second but couldn't keep up with Clijsters, who was playing some of the best tennis of her career. It was hard to imagine she had only been playing for a few months since her return.

The second set finished 6–3 to Clijsters, giving her a straight-sets win and her second US Open title! The victory made her the first unseeded player and the first wild card to win the US Open, the first mother to win a major since 1980, and it also shot her up the rankings to 19th in the world.

Incredibly, she returned the following year and won it again, showing that not only had 2009 not been a fluke but that she was back to the top of the game, and that is where she was going to stay. In that 2010 US Open, Kim beat Venus Williams in the semifinals, meaning she had beaten both sisters at the same stage two years running before dismantling Vera Zvonareva 6-2 6-1 in the final.

Kim continued to progress, winning the 2011 Australian Open the following year. It was her last singles major, bringing her total to four, which finally propelled her back to the number one ranking in the world, which her tennis had desperately deserved. It also gave her the joint record for most majors won by a mother—three.

In total, Kim won 41 singles titles in her career, including four majors. Between singles and doubles, she won all four Grand Slams, making her one of the most successful female players of the Open Era.

Kim Clijsters wasn't just a winner; she was pure class on the court. She was given many sportsmanship awards, and she always played with a smile on her face. Every crowd loved her, and along with Justine Henin, she is credited with making tennis one of the most popular sports in Belgium.

A mother, a champion, and a returning champion—it's easy to see why Kim Clijsters is known as a tennis great!

THE FAIRYTALE OF MARCUS WILLIS

Some of you may not have heard of Marcus Willis, and that's because he was never really in the majors or later rounds of smaller tournaments. In fact, he only ever made it to the main draw of a major once in singles and spent most of his career in the qualifying rounds and at lower-level tournaments like Challengers and Futures. However, that one main draw appearance at Wimbledon was one of the most special and unlikely that tennis has ever seen and thoroughly deserves its spot as one of the most incredible fairytale runs that tennis has ever seen.

Marcus Willis's story began in Slough, Berkshire, England, on October 9, 1990. As a kid, he liked most sports, but tennis was always his favorite. He began playing at 9, and from that point on, all he ever wanted to do was play on the professional tour. But his main dream was to step out onto Centre Court at Wimbledon. That dream would come true, but not before he had almost given up on it ever happening.

Although Marcus officially turned pro at 17, he didn't play his first ATP singles match until he was 26. He had some success in doubles, but he just couldn't seem to make the step up in singles. Marcus refused to accept that he would never be a singles player, and he entered every tournament he could, which usually meant trying to get through the qualifying rounds and playing in the lower levels of professional tennis.

He had his first shot at Wimbledon in 2009 when he was only 18. He was given a wild card into the qualifiers but failed to progress. Marcus reached his highest ranking in 2014 when he made it to 322 in the world, but of course, this was still not close to high enough to get him into any of the Grand Slams. By that point, he knew that he would never be one of the top players. In fact, he thought about retiring.

It was his girlfriend who talked him out of it. She told him he would regret it forever if he never reached the main draw of a major. Marcus kept trying, but over the next couple of years, his ranking slipped even further. Soon, he was outside the top 700.

His favorite player growing up was Roger Federer, who had blown up in the early 2000s while Marcus was a teenager. He took a lot of inspiration from the game of the Swiss legend, trying to apply it to his own to even reach a fraction of Roger's success in his career. When Marcus turned pro, it would always have been his dream to play against his idol, but of course, he wasn't ever going to play against Federer in any qualifying rounds or lower-level tournaments - he had to qualify for the main draw of one of the big ones.

Then, in 2016, something unbelievable started to unfold. Marcus, who was now ranked 772nd in the world, didn't have a chance of getting into the Wimbledon qualifiers due to his ranking, but the UK was hosting a pre-qualifiers tournament, where the winner got a spot in Wimbledon qualifying. Now, if you think Marcus' ranking was high enough to get into that, then guess again. He was actually the first alternate before a player pulled out at the last minute and gave Marcus the slightest glimmer of hope of playing on the grass at the All England Club, although he would have to win six matches in a row against players ranked hundreds of places above him to ever reach the main draw. Impossible, right?

He hadn't played competitive tennis for months, and it was a lot of effort to probably end up getting dumped out early. We only have to look at his earnings before the 2016 Wimbledon—$356—to show how badly Marcus's year had been going. Yep, that's right. Marcus Willis's total earnings were just $356!

Marcus decided to play. He trained like crazy, putting in as many hours on the court as he could squeeze in, and suddenly started playing the tennis of his life. Marcus has a very big serve and is good at the net, so his game is built for the fast grass courts. He played three outstanding matches against some of the brightest prospects in British tennis to win the pre-qualifiers and make it into Wimbledon qualifying. Now, the real challenge was about to begin.

After all that, the qualifying draw was made, and he was given possibly one of the hardest runs ever to reach the main draw. If he won his first round, he would have to play future top-5 player Andrey Rublev, and if he won that, he would have to play future world number one Daniil Medvedev.

Qualifying seemed impossible for a player ranked as low as Marcus, but as soon as the first round began, it was clear that he was a player on a mission, playing more like someone who was 100 in the world than someone barely in the top 1000. He beat Yūichi Sugita 1-6 6-4 6-1 in the first round, dispatched of Rublev 7-5 6-4 in the second, and came through a nailbiting final qualifying round against against Medvedev 3-6 7-5 6-3 6-4. Marcus had done the unthinkable and won six matches in a row to qualify!

Unlike in qualifying, Marcus was given a favorable draw in the main draw and was up against Lithuanian player Ricardas Berankis. However, what made this draw 100 times better is that, if he won, and this was a big if as Berankis was over 700 places above him in the rankings, he would get to play against his hero - Roger Federer. The lifelong dream that had seemed so impossible was now on the brink of happening.

Marcus played like a seasoned top-100 pro and crushed Berankis 6-3 6-3 6-4 to the delight of the crowd, who were going wild with every point that he won. The sheer joy on Marcus' face after the match was a delight for everyone to see as the true scale of what he had achieved sank in. Not only was he in the second round of Wimbledon, but it was going to be on Centre Court against Roger Federer!

The match against Federer proved a step too far for Marcus, with the Swiss maestro's class shining through. Marcus was cheered onto Centre Court, but at the end of the day, he was facing one of the greatest of all time. Wimbledon was Federer's house. He had won it seven times already, and he would do so again the following year. Centre Court was like a casual stroll in the park to him!

Federer won the match 6-0 6-3 6-4, but not before Marcus played a delicious lob that landed just inside the baseline and brought one of the loudest cheers of the day from the crowd. Even Federer stopped to clap his racket in respect. In fact, that lob was voted as the shot of the tournament.

As the players left, the crowd rose to their feet as one and clapped Marcus off the court. It was an emotional moment for him, as he had just lived out two of his biggest dreams in one go. He had played against Roger Federer, and he had done it on Centre Court.

Following Wimbledon, Marcus received more invitations to tournaments than he had ever had before. He was a minor celebrity on the Tour. Although he won a couple of small events, nothing ever came close to matching the day he brought the Centre Court crowd to their feet!

Not all dreams end with trophies and glory. Some of them mean more, such as a kid wanting to one day share a court with his idol, only to see it come true just when it seemed impossible. Marcus Willis got to live his dream, and his fairytale run at Wimbledon will always be remembered as one of the most magical moments in the tournament's long history!

LEGENDARY COMEBACKS

JENNIFER CAPRIATI: DOWN BUT NOT OUT

A great comeback is always so entertaining. When it looks like there is no way back for a player, but they still find a way to drag themselves to victory, it's a sight to behold. Of course, there is the collapse of the other player, the one who looked sure to win, which only adds to the drama!

Yes, comebacks are one of the things that make certain matches unforgettable.

One of those matches came on January 26, 2002, when Jennifer Capriati stormed back against Martina Hingis when it looked like the match was as good as over. To make it even more special, it was the Australian Open final and Capriati's final Grand Slam title!

Jennifer Capriati won three majors in her career and won gold at the 1992 Summer Olympics. Her ability to take the ball early changed the way tennis was played, and her return of serve is still considered one of the best in history. She was a tennis prodigy as a kid, and when we say prodigy, we really mean it! She is one of only nine players in history to win the junior Orange Bowl title twice, and turned pro shortly after her 13th birthday.

Soon after turning pro, and just after starting high

school, she was in her first WTA Tour final, which she narrowly lost to world No. 2 Gabriela Sabatini. Jennifer followed this up by becoming the youngest player to ever reach the semifinal of the French Open. Then, in 1992, she won gold at the Olympics. It was a lot to take in for a 16-year-old kid.

The sudden fame and demands of being a top player got the better of her for a while. Feeling like she might crack under the pressure, Jennifer retired from tennis in 1994. She was just 18.

After a two-year break, she returned to the sport she loved, but it looked like that spark had gone from her game. She didn't seem to have the same desire to win.

Jennifer didn't really make waves again until 2000, when she reached the semifinals of the Australian Open. It was seen as the return of the devastating player who had ripped it up in her teens. But her return to the top was only just beginning. She then won two Slams in 2001—the Australian Open and French Open—before becoming world No. 1 in October of that year.

Capriati had beaten Martina Hingis in straight sets in that 2001 Australian Open final, so when they met again in 2002, she was seen as the favorite. But it didn't start out that way, and before Jennifer knew what was happening, Hingis had won the first set 6-4.

Both players loved the Australian Open. Capriati had won there the previous year, while Hingis had won it three times in a row in 1997, '98, and '99. It was clear that a battle was on the cards!

The heat that day was insane, and both players were clearly exhausted after the first set. Hingis soon took control, rattling off a 4-0 lead in the second set. Jennifer looked well and truly beaten. She was letting the moment get to her, and she even began shouting at the crowd at one point, telling them to be quiet while the players were in action.

Almost like the flick of a switch, Jennifer suddenly changed into beast mode. At 0–4 and a double break down, she would have been forgiven for just accepting her fate and rolling over. Instead, she fired off three straight games and two breaks of serve to bring the score back to 3–4. The match was now back on serve, and momentum seemed to be with Jennifer, but amazingly, Hingis struck back. She broke Capriati's serve again and was suddenly one game away from the title and serving for it.

All went according to plan, and Hingis got herself to 40-30 and match point up. After a fantastic rally, where Hingis was on the front foot for much of it, Capriati produced a devastating backhand crosscourt winner to take the game back to deuce, before completing the comeback and breaking serve to bring it back to 4-5.

The two exchanged holds of serve until Capriati was 5-6 down and once again serving to stay in the championship. Martina played fantastic tennis to earn herself two more championship points, but to the astonishment of everyone watching, Jennifer was able to save them with some more pin-point groundstrokes.

The match headed to a tiebreak, but the drama wasn't done there. Hingis had her fourth championship point at 7-6 in the tiebreak, but after an agonizing rally where she sent a backhand just past the baseline, she was unable to win it again. Hingis, who had seemed absolutely certain to win the match 20 minutes ago, was now all over the place, muttering to herself in disbelief at what was happening. With the previous match points clearly on her mind, Hingis played a poor final two points, and the tiebreak went to Capriati.

Now, Capriati had all of the momentum*, and she knew it. She took control of the match, playing solid tennis as Martina started to self-destruct, winning the final set 6–2 to complete one of the greatest comebacks the Australian Open has ever seen. In fact, no player had ever saved four match points in the final of a Slam before. It was as close to a miracle as you could get!

Some commentators believe this defeat convinced Martina Hingis to retire. Actually, neither of them ever played in a Slam final again. They will both forever be legends of the game, though, and that final was the perfect way to sign off!

RAFA NADAL'S
UNBELIEVABLE TURNAROUND

Rafael "Rafa" Nadal played in many classic matches during his long, glittering career. For one match to stand out more than the rest, well, it has to be insane, right? That's exactly what his 2022 Australian Open victory over Daniil Medvedev was—it was utterly insane!

For one thing, Nadal was 35 and considered "past his prime." Not only was age catching up to him, but he had spent the majority of the previous six months out with a foot injury that had even stopped him from walking at times and looked almost sure to end his career. In fact, it wasn't as if Nadal's foot injury had recovered. He was instead having to take injections in his foot every time he played to deal with the pain, which meant that his time on court had been very limited in the build-up to the tournament.

The fact that he was even playing was a miracle, but no one expected much of the Spanish great. Just to make a deep run even more unlikely, the Australian Open had also been Nadal's weakest of the majors over the years. Yes, he had won it once in 2009, but for a player of Nadal's caliber, winning a major only one time comfortably made it his worst.

Medvedev and Nadal had a history. They had played

out an epic in the 2019 US Open final three years before, with Nadal just about coming out on top. They both knew the other player would throw everything that they had against them and that another epic battle was on the horizon.

Most of the Australian crowd were cheering for Nadal. It had been 13 years since his Australian Open victory, and with his age and horrific foot problems, everyone feared that it might be the last time that they saw him at the tournament, let alone in the final. It truly would be a fairytale run if he was able to go on to win it one more time.

A few months before the final, Medvedev had won his first Slam, the US Open. He was the in-form player and was looking to make it two Slams in a row. He was younger, fitter, and expected to win. Nadal had other plans.

The match started out like most people expected, with the younger player taking control. When he won five consecutive games in the first set to take it 6–2, the match looked dead and buried for Nadal. The second set was closer, and it went to a tiebreak, which Medvedev won 7–5 to give him a two sets to love lead and bring the match seemingly out of sight for Rafa.

That second set should have taken more out of the 35-year-old Nadal than it did Medvedev, yet it somehow seemed to ignite something in Rafa. He came out for the third set like a bull, his shoulders pulled back and a snarl on his face. Champions are built differently than regular folk, and Nadal was already a 20-time major winner. He knew he still had it in him, and he was determined to prove it to the world.

However, as the third set began, it seemed to be the same old story. Medvedev was holding serve easily while Nadal was struggling, and when Nadal went 0-40 down on his serve at 2-3 down in the third set, the match looked over. If Medvedev broke here, he would surely go on to win the title. But this is Nadal we're talking about, and he fights until the very end. Rafa roared back, still as hungry to win every point as ever, to hold serve and bring the momentum on his side. With a spring in his step and Medvedev looking rattled for the first time in the match, Nadal sent a monstrous backhand pass down the line to break the Russian's serve at 4-4 before holding his serve to love to take the third set 6-4.

The level in the fourth set was crazy, and it was clear Medvedev wanted to stop the comeback and close the match out here. Every rally seemed to defy what was possible on a court, and both players exchanged a break early in the set, but Rafa was like a caged bull at this point and could not be stopped. He broke Daniil for a second time at 2-2, and that was enough for Rafa to serve out the rest of the set and take it 6-4 and level the match at two sets all.

At the time, all of the Big Three (Nadal, Federer, and Djokovic) were tied on the all-time Grand Slam winners list with 20 wins each, which put even more pressure on this match. Not only was Rafa looking to become one of the oldest major winners in history, but he was also looking to take the solo lead as the greatest Grand Slam champion men's tennis has ever seen, ahead of the two other greatest players in history. This was surely racing through his mind as he sat down after clinching that incredible fourth set.

The drama continued in the fifth set, and it was Rafa who struck first. He sent a trademark whipped forehand down the line for an impossible winner to break Medvedev's serve to go 3-2 up, and the stage was set for him to win his 21st Grand Slam. But every epic match has one final twist, which came when Nadal was serving for the title at 5-4. Despite going 30-0 up, Medvedev produced some inspired tennis to win four points in a row and break Rafa's serve.

Many lesser players would let this get to them, but this is the great Rafael Nadal we are talking about, and a setback was never going to make him drop his level. In fact, it did the opposite. After some brutal rallies, Rafa broke straight back to give him his second chance at serving out the match. This time, he didn't slip up and held to love to win his 21st (and then-record) major.

Both players hugged it out. They knew they had just taken part in something special. Nadal had been a part of countless incredible victories in his long career, but to many, this one was the greatest. Given his age, his foot problems, and going two sets to love down, it certainly was his most unlikely.

HENRI COCHET:
WIMBLEDON'S FORGOTTEN HERO

During the 1920s and 1930s, four French players dominated tennis. They came through around the same time, and between them, they won pretty much everything there was to win. They were known as the "Four Musketeers," and they were fantastic.

One of the best of the bunch, Henri Cochet, represented everything good about the Four Musketeers. He was quick, strong, a true winner, and he never knew when he was beaten. During his amazing career, he won all three Slams (there were only three back then, not four), including four French Opens, two Wimbledons, and one US Open. He also won silver in both the doubles and singles events at the 1924 Paris Olympics.

Of all the major tournaments he won, his performance at Wimbledon in 1927 was the best. He showed his fighting spirit not once, not twice, but three times on his way to winning the tournament!

Henri was born in Villeurbanne, France, in 1901. At the time, tennis was strictly for the very rich. It wasn't really the type of sport played on the street. Henri's family was far from rich, but luckily for him, his father was a groundskeeper at the Lyonnaise tennis club. As a kid, Henri used to join his father at work, where he earned court time by helping out as a ball boy when the adults played.

His talents were spotted pretty quickly, and he was soon being trained by the club's president and professionally ranked player, Georges Cozon. Henri didn't have to work for his court time anymore!

Henri quickly earned a name as an up-and-coming star. At the time, France was beginning a golden age of tennis. They had more young prospects than they knew what to do with. In a few years, the Four Musketeers would be unleashed on the world!

In one local tournament, Henri actually faced his coach and hero, Georges Cozon, in the final. Henri won, and Georges knew it was time to let his student take a shot at the big time. Henri was ready to turn pro!

All Four Musketeers had periods where they dominated on their own. Henri's began in 1926 when he won the French Open. This was soon followed by his miraculous Wimbledon run. It was also the beginning of the period when French players ruled tennis.

When the 1927 Wimbledon began, Henri was ranked 4th in the world. During his run, he knocked out the two top-seeded Americans, Frank Hunter and Bill Tilden. What makes these matches special, apart from the fact that they were the quarter and semifinals of Wimbledon, is the way in which Henri won them.

In both matches, he was two sets to love down, each

time coming back to win the match in five sets. Each match was an epic, and they dragged on for a long time, meaning Henri was exhausted by the time he played the final. In the semifinal against legendary player Tilden, Henri nearly lost in straight sets, and this incredible story would have been over before it started. He saved several match points in the third set before eventually winning it 7–5, before winning the next two sets 6–4, 6–3.

When he met fellow Musketeer Jean Borotra in the final, it was expected to be a classic, and it was. In fact, it is still seen as one of the best Wimbledon finals in history.

Henri was looking to win his first Wimbledon, whereas Borotra had won it twice already. He was the reigning champion, having won it the previous year, so he knew what it took to carry himself to victory.

Borotra had played through an epic in the semifinals himself, with the match going the full five sets. The difference was that Borotra had held a two-set lead, only to drop the third and fourth sets before coming through in the decider. Either way, it showed he also had bags of fighting spirit. Both players would need every drip of moxie they could muster for the final!

Much like the previous two rounds, Henri would go two sets down in the final. And once again, he came roaring back to win! His record of winning three Grand Slam matches in a row from two sets to love down stood until the 2013 French Open when it was matched by Tommy Robredo. Nobody has ever beaten it.

The match was close from start to finish. Borotra won the first set 6–4 and then repeated the same score in the second. Once again, Henri was two sets down, but this is where he thrived. He picked himself up and powered back, winning the third set 6–3. When he won the fourth set 6-4, Borotra looked stunned. He knew about Henri's incredible comebacks in the previous rounds and must have been in disbelief that it was happening again.

The fifth set was an all-time classic. Despite having six championship points, Borotra could not put the match away, and Henri won the decider 7-5. Somehow, defying all the odds, he had won the match in five sets and won his first Wimbledon title. His opponent and friend was devastated, but he knew he had taken part in a match for the ages. Borotra knew how hard it was to win Wimbledon, having done it twice himself. He was surely proud of his fellow countryman.

Henri broke another record in that match. He was the first (and still the only) player to win a Grand Slam final after saving six match points. If that doesn't show his passion and fighting spirit, then nothing does!

To come back from two sets down in any match is special. But to do it in a quarterfinal, semifinal, and final of a major, well, that's pretty much a sporting miracle!

NOVOTNA'S HEARTBREAK, RUBIN'S TRIUMPH

This one feels a little different from the rest, but only because the player who lost had thrown away a big lead a couple of years beforehand. Of course, Chanda Rubin had to give everything she had to mount her comeback, but questions will always be asked about Jana Novotna's ability to close out matches.

Long, drawn-out matches were something of a specialty for Chanda. She was not only involved in the epic comeback we're about to cover, but she was also part of the longest match in women's singles in Wimbledon history. She won both matches, which kind of proves that her victory over Novotna was probably more about Chanda's fighting spirit than her opponent choking!

Her brilliant match against Novotna came at Roland-Garros on June 3, 1995. It was the third round of the French Open, on clay, and Chanda was just 19. Novotna was ranked 5th in the world and looking to win her first major. Her day would come a few years later when she was victorious at Wimbledon, but that day, at the French Open, Chanda Rubin had other plans!

One of Jana Novotna's weaker points was her temperament*. She often found herself getting dragged into arguments with umpires and people in the crowd. When this happened, her anger took over, and she lost control of her matches. Chanda was aware of this going into the match, and she used it to her advantage.

Two years previously, Jana had thrown away a huge lead in the final of Wimbledon. She lost the match 5–7, 6–1, 4–6, which seems pretty close until you realize that after winning the second set 6–1 and then taking a 4–1 lead in the decider, she double-faulted on game point to make it 5–1. She then lost the game and every other one after that to lose the match 6-4 in the third set.

Chanda later admitted that the Wimbledon final was in her head as she started her own comeback at the French Open. She knew that deep down, surely Novotna was also thinking about it and probably terrified that she might choke again.

Still, Novotna was the heavy favorite. She was ranked 5th in the world, and her opponent was still an up-and-coming teenager. But sometimes youth can blind the younger players, as they go into big matches with no fear. They know their whole career is ahead of them, so they take more risks. So what if it doesn't work out? They'll be back many more times, right?

It was Chanda who took the lead, winning a grueling first set 7–6. That opening set took a lot out of both players. It was a hot day, and clay is the most draining of all surfaces. The courts are slow and high-bouncing, and as the matches progress and the balls get fluffier and heavier, it can leave both players exhausted.

After arguing with the umpire, Novotna settled herself enough to win the second set 6–4. In the third set, she caught fire, winning the first five games to take a 5–0 lead and leave herself just one game away from victory. It looked like Chanda's race was run. To make matters worse, Novotna stormed to a 40-0 lead at 5-0, and the match was over, right? I mean, Novotna is 5-0 40-0 up. How can this story possibly continue?

Well, to the surprise of everyone watching, Rubin started clawing points back, and from the brink of defeat, she won the game to go to 5-1. Still, even at 5-1 in the third, Novotna was still in complete control. Or so it seemed. More match points came and went, and slowly but surely, Chanda was coming back. The energy from the court spread through the crowd, and Novotna could feel it. Once again, she started complaining and cursing under her breath.

Everyone believed the match was over at 5–0 in the third set. Even Lindsay Davenport, who was next on the court, had gotten herself ready to come out. Her rackets were packed, and she was standing on the sidelines waiting for the call! Then Chanda won two, three, four games in a row!

Novotna squandered her ninth match point at 5-4, before Chanda drew the scores level at 5-5. Yes, you read that right. She had nine match points and failed to win any! The tension around the court was unbearable, with both the players and fans in disbelief at what was happening. Just 15 minutes before, they had been watching a routine third round win for the world number five, but now they were witnessing perhaps the worst choke in tennis history.

Novotna's shoulders slumped and Chanda could sense that her opponent was not only weakened but completely distraught. Impressively, Novotna regained some composure to take the match to 6-6, but there was only ever going to be one winner at this point. Chanda showed Novotna how to serve out a match and won the final two games to win the decider 8-6.

At just 19 years old, and despite being ranked 48 places lower than her opponent, Rubin had come back from 0-5 0-40 down in the deciding set, saving nine match points, to win the unlikeliest of matches.

Unfortunately, the insane match had taken a lot out of Chanda. She managed to reach the quarterfinals, but she was drained mentally and physically. As for Jana Novotna, she ended up earning an unfortunate and slightly unfair reputation as a choker. Yes, she suffered some horrendous defeats from winning positions, but she retired as a Wimbledon champion and 12-time doubles major winner, so it's safe to say that her nerves were just fine for most of her career.

Chanda Rubin never really reached the heights that were expected, but she still won seven professional tournaments, as well as winning the Australian Open in doubles. Sometimes, moments are just as memorable as medals. Chanda Rubin played in and won the longest match in the history of women's tennis at Wimbledon, as well as completing one of the greatest comebacks in French Open history.

That makes her a legend of the game!

TIMELESS
TENNIS
CLASSICS

FEDERER VS NADAL
THE GREATEST MATCH EVER PLAYED

Is there a more iconic rivalry in tennis than Federer and Nadal? Yes, Djokovic fans will certainly be saying something right now, but before the Serb rose to the top, these two were the kings of tennis. You have 'The King of Clay' Rafa Nadal, who was absolutely unstoppable at the French Open, and then you have the majestic Federer, whose elegant game and pin-point serve made him look impossible to beat on the grass at Wimbledon.

The pair had some epic battles over the years (40, to be exact), but their most interesting often took place when one challenged the other on their favorite surface. When they met in the Wimbledon final in 2008, Federer was on a run of five consecutive Wimbledon titles. But after a tight five-set victory over Nadal the year before, for the first time, it looked like Rafa had a chance of challenging on the grass.

And challenge he did! Over almost five hours of playing, the two produced some of the greatest tennis the sport has ever seen. That final is often considered the greatest match of all time, or at least the greatest in the modern era, and is etched into the minds of any tennis fans old enough to remember it.

Federer and Nadal had been so dominant in the years before the 2008 final that it seemed like they were the only two players in the world. Between them, they had won 14 of the previous 16 majors, with Federer being crowned champion ten of those times and the other four going to Rafa. Djokovic had recently won his first major at the Australian Open in 2008, but he was very much still the young up-and-coming player, and it would be a few years yet until the dominant two became the 'Big Three'.

Federer was also looking to break Bjorn Borg's record of five consecutive Wimbledon titles, having won his fifth the previous year. Federer was always going to be a legend of Wimbledon, no matter if he never won there again, but if could win the tournament six times in a row, he could be almost certain that it would be an achievement that no one else would ever match in the history of tennis. The 2008 final was set up to be an all-time classic.

Nadal was also in top form. He had won the French Open (his fourth in a row) a few months before, and he was more than ready to win his first major on another surface! With tensions higher than they had been for a final in decades, the temperature only went up when rain delayed the start of the match right before it was about to begin.

When the match finally started, Nadal took off like a rocket. He won the first set 6–4 and then rattled off five consecutive games in the second set after falling 1–4 behind to win the second by the same scoreline. Rafa had a two-set lead!

If Rafa had been playing anyone other than Federer, he would have believed the match was as good as over.

But he was playing a Wimbledon legend who never knew when he was beaten. Federer stormed back, winning the third set 7–6 after another 80-minute rain delay. He repeated the feat in the fourth set to level the match.

That fourth set tiebreak is seen as the point in time when both players clashed at their peak. It was an endless stream of ridiculous passes, incredible winners, and out-of-this-world gets that are sure to give any tennis fan goosebumps anytime they watch it. Nadal even had two championship points in the breaker at 7-6 and 8-7, but Federer saved the first with a great serve and the second with one of the most incredible backhand passes of all time. Nadal played a phenomenal tiebreak that would have been good enough to close out any other match in tennis history, but Federer's was better. That's how high the level was.

By 19:53, the match was tied at two sets, and everyone was biting their nails in anticipation of what was sure to be another sensational set of tennis. Another rain delay just before the decider only added to the tension. Both players had to return to the locker room with nothing but their thoughts for company. For Federer, he knew he was one set away from winning six Wimbledons in a row! As for Rafa, he must have believed his chance was slipping away. He had just lost a two sets to love lead against the greatest player Wimbledon has ever seen, and to make matters worse, he'd had two championship points in the fourth set.

The players returned to the court half an hour later. It had gotten dark, and there was talk of the match being called off until the following day, but they played on under the lights. Suspending play would have been awful, as the players and crowd were as pumped as they were ever going to be. The match needed to be finished there and then!

The fifth and final set was as close as all the others. It was another epic. Both players ran themselves into the ground, with neither of them dropping their serve until right at the end. It was Federer who finally slipped up, eventually dropping serve in the 15th game to make it 8-7 to Nadal. As Rafa did countless times later in his career, he dealt with the pressure perfectly to serve out the match in a tight final game to finally get his hands on the Wimbledon trophy.

It was 21:15 by the time the match finished, having lasted four hours and 48 minutes, and that's not including the rain delays! In fact, it was the last final to be properly affected by rain, as the now-famous retractable roof was installed before the 2009 tournament.

Roger Federer would reclaim his crown the following year, only for Nadal to win it again in 2010! Novak Djokovic soon took over as the Wimbledon top dog, winning seven titles between 2011 and 2022. He was also involved in many epics of his own, but none have quite been able to match that legendary match in 2008 that will undoubtedly live on forever in tennis history.

GRAF VS NAVRATILOVA
A FRENCH OPEN EPIC

Steffi Graf and Martina Navratilova are two of the greatest players in the history of tennis. In fact, both can make a good claim to being the greatest player ever. Steffi went on to win 22 Grand Slam singles titles, and Martina went on to win 18 in singles and 41 major titles in doubles and mixed doubles. Both had ridiculously good careers, but when they met in 1987, Steffi Graf was the new kid on the block. She was trying to knock Navratilova off the top. Graf was 13 years younger, but what Navratilova lacked in youth, she more than made up for in experience.

Both players had a history with one another. A year before, at the 1986 US Open, they met in a bruising semifinal, which was such a good match that it could easily have made this list. At the time, Navratilova was world No. 1, and the 17-year-old Graf was No. 3. It was seen as the teacher versus the student. That day, the teacher won!

Graf wanted revenge. In that semifinal at the US Open, she had chances to finish Navratilova off. In fact, Graf had three match points before Navratilova's experience prevailed, and she ground down her younger opponent and won. Navratilova went on to lift the trophy!

By the time they met at Roland-Garros, Graf had

moved up one place to world No. 2. Still, the wily Navratilova was still No. 1, and she intended to stay there for a while yet!

Steffi Graf was 18 and yet to win a Slam. Navratilova had dominated the women's game for a decade. The French Open final was set up to be a classic. Graf started well, winning the first set 6–4. She had held a lead over Navratilova and lost before, so she was taking nothing for granted. And rightly so. Navratilova used all of her experience to fight back in the second set, winning it 6–4, to once again bring the match to a decider.

The third set is where it really ramped up!

Both players were playing devastating tennis, coming to the net as much as possible, but no matter how well one played, the other always had an answer. Both players remained rock-solid behind their serves, until suddenly, in the seventh game, cracks started to emerge in the young German's tennis. Navratilova capitalized on some slack points to break Steffi's serve and, after a swift hold, moved 5-3 up. It seemed that Steffi had come so close again, only for the experience of Navratilova to pull through when it mattered most.

Graf held her nerve the following game to hold and bring the decider back to 4-5, but now it was Navratilova's turn to try to serve out the match. However, the usually calm Navratilova suddenly started to feel the pressure. Very uncharacteristically, she started to let the game slip away, and after a double fault to make it 15-40, she gave Steffi two lifelines back into the match. Graf only needed one as she broke back to come back from the brink of defeat and bring the decider level at 5-5.

Navratilova carried on battling, but the power and energy from Steffi proved too much. Graf played some phenomenal tennis, hitting two stunning passes to break Navratilova when she was serving to stay in the match and clinch the decider 8-6.

Not only had she won her first major, but she had done it against one of the greatest champions in the history of tennis and had come back from 5-3 down in the decider! If that's not a classic, I don't know what it is.

This was a milestone victory that slowly started passing on the crown for the queen of tennis from Navratilova to Graf. However, that doesn't mean that the two didn't have many more epics after this, with Martina always putting up a big fight every time she stepped onto court. In fact, they met at that year's Wimbledon final, with Navratilova getting the victory.

The pair clashed 18 times over their careers, with the players sharing the wins with nine each. As for finals, they met in six, and Graf had the slightly better record of 4–2, but almost every one was a battle for the ages.

One of their best matches came years later at the 1991 US Open. Graf was world No.1 and the most dominant player in women's tennis at the time, while an aging Navratilova had slipped down to No. 6. So it was seen as a shock when Navratilova rolled back the years and beat Graf 7–6, 6–7, 6–4 to reach the final!

The Navratilova-Graf rivalry is one of the best ever. There might have been a big age difference, but that only made their matches more interesting. It added spice to what was already a tense, hardcore matchup! They played out some of the best matches tennis has ever seen, but their epic clash at the 1987 French Open final has to be the best!

ISNER VS MAHUT
THE ENDLESS MATCH

Not all of the greatest tennis matches involve the greatest tennis players. Sometimes, two slightly lesser-known players on one of the outer courts can play out a classic. One of those times, John Isner and Nicolas Mahut battled each other in what is now known as "The Endless Match."

In total, the whole match lasted three days! That includes the match being stopped at night and restarting the following afternoon, of course, but still! And even without darkness breaks, the actual match time was 11 hours and five minutes. The final set alone lasted eight hours and 11 minutes, as both players put on serving masterclasses and were impossible to break.

To go through every turning point in the match would be impossible. Isner and Mahut both played and served the best of their lives that day (or days!). It was just unfortunate for each of them that they came up against each other at the very moment. To give an idea of just how huge each player was serving during The Endless Match, we only have to look at the fact that both hit over 100 aces!

When they met in the first round of Wimbledon in 2010, both players were well-known and respected pros, but neither was ever considered a title contender, and rightly so. Mahut would go on to be a legendary doubles player later in his career, winning five Grand Slam titles, but at the time was a struggling singles player who had to come through qualifying. Isner was a more established singles player, being ranked 23 in the world, and went on to have a fantastic career, but at the time was still seen as a bit of an outsider. However, they both had one aspect of their games that was world-class, and that was, of course, their serves. And when two players with world-class serves face off on the fast courts at Wimbledon, matches can get very long, but no one was ready for what these two were about to do.

Their match was played on Court 18, one of the outer courts, and just had a sprinkling of people watching at the start. By the third day, there was so much hype and excitement around the match that people were queuing up all day just to get a glimpse of the history that the two players were making.

This was nine years before the 2019 rule change that forced the final set into a tiebreak if the score was 12–12. That has been shortened even more since, but back in 2010, the final set wasn't decided until one player won by two clear games. That meant it could officially continue forever if the players kept holding serve, and for a while, it looked like it would.

Grass was arguably Isner's best surface, with the 6 ft 10 American going on to make the semifinals at Wimbledon in the future, so he came into the match as the heavy favorite and expecting to win fairly comfortably. The match started as expected, and Isner won the first set 6-4, but surprisingly, Mahut came roaring back. The Frenchman won the second set 6-3 and then took a tight third set in a tiebreak. Isner showed his class by bouncing back in the fourth set to win it 7-6, and the match that was expected to be relatively one-sided was going the full five sets. It was already late into the night as the fourth set ended, so the match was halted until the following day, but what the players could never have dreamed of is that in two days time, they would be sitting in the same spot with the match still not finished!

As the players and fans came back onto court the following day, it just seemed like a tight but normal match that would be over in less than an hour. How wrong they were!

They came out like players possessed, putting on one of the best serving masterclasses that tennis has ever seen. Although there had been two breaks of serve the previous day, it suddenly seemed like it would be impossible for either player to break through on their serve. The pair kept trading games, but at 10-9 to Isner, he had his first opening. After some fantastic returning, he orchestrated a breakpoint at 30-40, but in classic fashion, Mahut saved it with an ace, and the match continued.

Matches generally started to get noticed around the grounds once they went past 10-10 in the fifth set, as this is already rare, but when it went to 20-20, people knew that something historic was happening. By the time the next match point came, they had already smashed the previous fifth-set games record, with Isner leading 33-32. Yes, you read that right! This time Isner went 15-40 up on the Mahut serve, but once again, the Frenchman showed nerves of steel to save the first with a fantastic volley, before sending down another thundering unreturnable serve to save the second. And the match carried on...

Mahut finally had his turn at a pair of break points when Isner was serving at 50-50, but the American did what he did best and served his way out of trouble to hold serve. Then followed hold after hold until, at 58-59 on the Mahut serve, daylight was fading and it seemed that he just needed to hold serve one more time to bring the match into its third day. But Isner sensed his opportunity and, despite being so tired that he could barely stand up, was able to get his fourth championship point. The crowd were going crazy with every point, always rooting for the history-making match to go on longer, and they got their wish once again. Mahut sent down another devastating ace down the tee and held serve to bring it to 59-59.

Despite chants from the spectators saying, "We want more, we want more," the umpire had no choice but to suspend the match until the following day. By this point, every tennis fan in the world had stopped what they were doing to tune into the match that was making history at Wimbledon. No one had ever even gone past 30-30 in a final set before, and yet here they were, halting play at 59-59. Breaking the record was incredible, but it was simply beyond belief that they could break it by this many games. In fact, both players looked so unbreakable behind their serves that many fans thought the match might even go on to 100-100, or never even end, for that matter.

They began the third day looking tired but just as determined as they continued to smash down aces and rattle off service hold after hold. It actually seemed to be Isner who was struggling more physically, but against the run of play, he was able to generate his fifth match point with the score at 68-69 and 30-40. He had a different look in his eyes this time. It was the look of a man who knew that he had to win this point, or else his body would completely give up on him, and he would surely lose the match. Mahut fired down a trademark big serve out wide, but this time, Isner connected well with the return, and after a tough half-volley from Mahut, Isner sent a roaring backhand pass down the line to win the match and sink to the court in relief.

Isner won the final set 70-68 in a match that lasted 11 hours and 5 minutes and took three days to complete. It was a true depiction of the word battle and was loved and cheered on by millions of fans worldwide. Naturally, Isner was absolutely shattered after the match, and was a shell of himself as he could barely walk during a 6-0 6-3 6-2 second round defeat, but he had been a part of one of the most iconic matches in Grand Slam history, and if you asked him to this day whether it was worth it or not, he would surely say that it absolutely was.

Since then, the rules have been changed, and matches have to go to tiebreaks in fifth sets. It is now virtually impossible for The Endless Match to ever be equaled. It is a record that is well and truly deserved by both players and will surely stand forever!

BORG VS MCENROE
THE GREATEST TIEBREAK EVER

Few rivalries can match the one between Bjorn Borg and John McEnroe. It was a professional rivalry and a personal one. They really didn't like each other, and the crowd couldn't get enough of it. Bjorn Borg was the perfect professional, a winner who practiced hard and never spoke out of turn. John McEnroe was the bad boy, the villain, the man who made arguing with umpires popular! It was the perfect rivalry for TV audiences.

This fire and ice* rivalry began in 1978 and only really lasted until 1981. In that time, they met 14 times, with both players sharing seven victories each. They just couldn't be separated. Bjorn Borg was three years older and the original king of Wimbledon. He had won the event four years running before that 1980 Wimbledon final, and he was looking to make it five. McEnroe had yet to win it!

By 1980, Borg had become so dominant in the French Open and Wimbledon that it felt like nobody else would win until he retired. Surprisingly, he never won either of the other two Slams (US Open and Australian Open), but he was basically unbeatable at Roland-Garros and Wimbledon.

The 1980 final was McEnroe's first time getting that far, and he was up against the man who had won the last four! Their rivalry had started before then, so tensions were high. For added spice, Borg was world No. 1, and McEnroe was No. 2. It was set up to be an epic!

In the previous round, a semifinal classic between McEnroe and Jimmy Connors, McEnroe had flipped out several times, slamming his racket, shouting at the umpire, and cursing at the crowd. It had made the fans turn against him, and as he walked out onto Centre Court for the final, he was met by a wall of boos! It was a reaction John McEnroe would get used to throughout his career.

McEnroe used the hate to spur him on. He started the match in beast mode, demolishing Borg 6–1 in the opening set. Borg hit back in the second, using his cool, calm attitude to frustrate McEnroe, winning the second set 7-5.

The third set saw Borg extend his lead, this time winning 6–3. McEnroe was visibly annoyed, and the crowd waited excitedly for him to explode. Instead, and rather uncharacteristically, he gathered himself and won one of the most epic and historic sets in the history of tennis. In fact, it is a set that was of such a high standard that many believe it is the best ever played.

Nothing could separate the players after twelve games, with both players serving and volleying phenomenally, and the match headed to a tiebreak. As true champions always do when it counts most, both stepped up to the plate to produce points of the highest quality, hitting outrageous drop shots, passes, and volleys to the amazement of the crowd. Match points came and went for Borg, but every time he went ahead, McEnroe produced a moment of brilliance to bring the scores level. In fact, Borg had five championship points as the tiebreak kept getting longer and longer, but in the end, it was McEnroe who clinched the classic 18-16 in the breaker, and the match was headed for a decider.

The final set was another war, and by this point, the crowd had completely forgotten their dislike of McEnroe, and were instead cheering both players on with every stunning winner they hit. It was Borg's steady, machine-like play against McEnroe's rock 'n' roll chance-taking Hollywood attitude, and they couldn't get enough.

In the end, Borg's serve proved too strong for McEnroe, and the Swede took the tense decider 8-6. It was his fifth Wimbledon in a row, and he had stopped the steam train that was McEnroe in an epic that everyone knew would live on in tennis history forever. Even so, he must have known his younger opponent would have his day. John McEnroe was just too good to be held back.

The following year, McEnroe returned to London, desperate to go one step further and win Wimbledon. The 1980 final still hurt, and he wanted to make things right. By now, some of the crowd on Centre Court had started to come around to the loud-mouthed American. They liked his passion and loved his style of play. When he came up against Borg in the final once more, it became one of the most anticipated* matches in history.

McEnroe won the 1981 final to lift his first Wimbledon trophy. He stopped Borg from winning his sixth in a row, and he also ended the Swede's 41 consecutive match streak at Wimbledon. They met again soon after in the final of the US Open, with McEnroe coming out on top once more. That loss infuriated Borg, who stormed out of the venue and didn't even stick around for the ceremonies.

Bjorn Borg never really recovered from the US Open defeat and, to the shock of the world, retired soon after.

Unlike the Federer-Nadal rivalry or the Djokovic-Nadal-Federer rivalry, where there was a quiet respect for each other, the McEnroe-Borg rivalry was openly fierce. The things they said about each other and how they stared each other down on the court made it much more entertaining.

In the years after both of their retirements, Bjorn Borg and John McEnroe have actually become quite close. Even when they hated each other, they respected how good the other player was. They knew they brought the best out in each other.

Several of the matches between Borg and McEnroe could have made this Greatest Matches list, but the 1980 final had everything. It was the good guy against the pantomime villain. The no-nonsense Swede versus the cocky American. It was everything that makes tennis great, and it didn't disappoint!

COOL DOWN

So, there you have it. You've finished reading about some of the most inspiring players and moments in the history of tennis. As you probably noticed, there was no way every inspiring moment or epic comeback, fairy-tale run, or best match could fit into the book. There have been too many.

Another thing you might have noticed is that the individual stories aren't numbered. That's simply because they can't be prioritized. Who's to say that Coco Gauff's story is more inspirational than Monica Seles', or is it the other way around? Or who can possibly decide which Wimbledon final was more epic —Borg versus McEnroe or Nadal versus Federer? The same goes for all the comebacks mentioned.

Fairy-tale runs are the same way. Just look at Michael Chang and Goran Ivanisevic. One was a kid when he won his only Slam, while the other was at the very end of his career. Which is harder to do? The young player has his fitness and power, but the older player is more experienced and knows how these things work!

Well, now it's up to you to decide which story goes where. It's a personal experience when we pick our favorite moments in sport, and it's great fun!

Did you get inspired while reading? Hopefully you did in some way. Inspiration is an excellent tool. It helps us to better ourselves, and that's always a positive. Who can say there was never a time when they suddenly wanted to train harder after watching a brilliant match on TV? Or how many of us have decided on the spot that we want to one day play at Wimbledon after seeing our favorite player win an epic match on Centre Court?

Inspiration can come in many forms. Just ask your parents if they wanted to be a boxer after watching the Rocky movies in the 1980s. You can bet that at least one of them went running as soon as they left the movie theater!

Some of the players covered in this book are still playing, so their stories continue to be told. Most of them are retired, though, so they have a beginning and an end. All of them achieved amazing things, even the few who never won Slams. People like Mansour Bahrami are amazing because they lived their dreams despite all of the horrors and hurdles that tried to block their way.

There are also the trailblazers, the people who pushed through horrible stuff like racism and sexism to leave the door open for others to follow. They made it easier for those who came after. Players such as Arthur Ashe broke down boundaries for the likes of Serena and Venus Williams to come after him. And Billie Jean King fought sexism and homophobia throughout her career. These people are legends of the game before we even look in their stacked trophy cabinets. They are legends of life!

Thankfully, most of the matches and moments can be

found online. YouTube has footage of the epic finals and battles mentioned, and there have even been Hollywood movies made about the Battle of the Sexes and the McEnroe-Borg rivalry. There is an endless stream of amazing shots and clashes to enjoy!

But there is something special in reading about it. When we picture it in our head, it makes it more personal. When we learn something new through reading, it sticks with us. We have it forever. Also, knowledge and learning keep us sharp. All top sports people will tell you that a sharp mind helps keep a sharp body, and vice versa*.

One of the great things about tennis is that it is played all year round. There is always a tournament or team event to enjoy, as well as the four majors. Tennis has a long history, too, which means there are always records to break and leaderboards to top! It makes everything all the more entertaining.

So, now it's time for you to grab your racket and ball and practice your game. Who knows, maybe one day, you'll be covered in a book just like this one! The next Novak Djokovic and Serena Williams are out there somewhere, so why can't it be you? Good luck!

GLOSSARY

Academic - An academic usually refers to someone who is a teacher or a college professor. It is someone who works in education.

Activism - Activists work hard to win rights or help certain views and charities, usually through protests, etc.

Agile - Able to stretch or bend easily. A yoga instructor or ballet dancer will be agile, for example.

All-court - An all-court player will be strong in every aspect of tennis, i.e., from the baseline, the net, defensively, and offensively.

All England Club - The club where Wimbledon is played.

Anticipated - To predict something is going to happen, then act on it.

Baiting - In sports, it can mean to lure the opponent into mistakes or a reaction, usually by getting under their skin.

Career Golden Masters - When a player wins all nine ATP Masters tournaments during their career. Novak Djokovic is the only player in history to achieve this!

Career Golden Slam - When a player wins all four majors and a gold medal at the Olympics during their career.

Career Grand Slam - When a player wins all four majors during their career.

Counter-puncher - A player who sits back and uses their opponent's pace to turn defense to attack after being out-of-position on the court. Counter-punchers usually move very well and hit very good groundstrokes on the run.

Citizenship - To become a legal citizen of any country where you weren't born, you need to earn citizenship.

Croquet - A sport played on short grass, where the players use mallets to knock hard wooden balls through hoops or wickets.

Exemplary - Perfect behavior or talent.

Fire and ice - Hot and cold. In this instance, it meant John McEnroe's temper (fire) and Bjorn Borg's calmness (ice).

Foot-fault - This is where a player's shoe is either touching or is over the baseline when they make contact with a serve. If this happens, it is considered an unfair advantage, so it doesn't count as a serve.

Hounded - Chased down, harassed.

Humility - Being modest and not thinking too much of yourself.

Limelight - To be the main focus.

Momentum - To gather pace. In sports, it can mean to start taking control of the match.

Nimble - Quick and light in movement.

Prodigy - A child who is exceptional at something.

Sexism - To treat someone differently because of their gender.

Sibling - A brother or sister.

Slap on the wrist - To get away with something with the minimum punishment.

Sportsmanship - To play fairly.

Starstruck - To be in awe of someone, usually someone famous.

Temperament - How someone controls their emotions.

Tiananmen Square Massacre - In 1989, hundreds of Chinese students who were protesting were killed by the Chinese army.

Vice versa - The same as the other way around.

Visa - The paperwork a person needs to stay in another country for a certain amount of time.

Western - This usually means most of Western Europe, North America, and Australasia.

Yugoslavia - A former country that broke up in 1992 and became Bosnia and Herzegovina, North Macedonia, Croatia, Montenegro, and Serbia.

Printed in Great Britain
by Amazon

60133285R00067